JESUS REDISCOVERED

Born in 1903, Malcolm Muggeridge was educated at Selhurst Grammar School and Selwyn College, Cambridge. He started his career as a university lecturer at the university in Cairo before taking up journalism. As a journalist he has worked around the world on the *Guardian*, *Calcutta Statesman*, the *Evening Standard* and the *Daily Telegraph*, and then in 1953 became editor of *Punch* where he remained for four years. His war service record as a Major in the Intelligence Corps was distinguished; he was awarded both the Légion d'Honneur and the Croix de Guerre.

In recent years Malcolm Muggeridge has become best known as a broadcaster both on television and radio and has not only contributed to such programmes as 'The Late Show' but has also done a series of documentaries for the B.B.C.

Collins have published two collections of his pieces: *Tread Softly for You Tread on My Jokes* in 1966 and a new edition of *The Thirties* in 1967.

MALCOLM MUGGERIDGE

JESUS REDISCOVERED

'O that thou shouldst give dust a tongue
To crie to thee.'
GEORGE HERBERT

Collins

FOUNT PAPERBACKS

First published in Fontana Books 1969
Thirteenth Impression March 1977
Reprinted in Fount Paperbacks May 1979

© 1969 Malcolm Muggeridge

Made and printed in Great Britain by
William Collins Sons & Co Ltd Glasgow

To my companion on the Road to Emmaus,
Allan Frazer

CONTENTS

FOREWORD

It is with the utmost trepidation and diffidence that I have collected together these miscellaneous pieces all directly or indirectly concerned with my attitude towards, and feelings about, the Christian religion. They do not set out to present a coherent, or even consistent, statement of faith. I am well aware that they are often contradictory, repetitive and imprecise; I have deliberately refrained from trying to trim and prune them into conveying an impression of coherence and consistency which would falsify my own actual mental state. All they represent—and it's little enough—is the effort of one ageing twentieth-century mind to give expression to a deep dissatisfaction with prevailing twentieth-century values and assumptions, and a sense that there is an alternative—an alternative propounded two thousand years ago by the Sea of Galilee and on the hill called Golgotha.

The theological implications of this position, I should explain, are quite beyond me. Theology is one of those subjects, like algebra and thermodynamics, in which I have never been able to interest myself. I am a theological ignoramus, and likely to remain one to the end of my days. Saintly and lion-hearted men, I know, have died heroically for concepts like the Trinity and the Virgin Birth which stir no more partisanship in me, one way or the other, than, say, the enchanting story of the creation in the Book of Genesis. All I can find to say for the Genesis version is that it strikes me as more plausible than Professor Hoyle's, and I certainly find the Virgin Birth as a notion more sympathetic than, say, family planning. Otherwise, St Thomas Aquinas and the Fathers must, I fear, remain for ever beyond my reach. My own masters (as readers will soon discover, I trust not to the point of tedium, from the frequency with which I quote them) have been a cherished few—the Gospels, of course, and the Epistles, especially St Paul's, the ever-beloved St Augus-

tine and St Francis, Bunyan and Blake, Pascal and Kierkegaard, Tolstoy and Dostoevsky. Bonhoeffer and, to me, the most
luminous intelligence of our time, Simone Weil. These have
taught me all I know—such as it is—of what I believe is called
Christian apologetics.

It was while I was in the Holy Land for the purpose of making three B.B.C. television programmes on the New Testament that a curious, almost magical, certainty seized me about
Jesus' birth, ministry and Crucifixion. I realised, in the first
place, that the many shrines, and the legends associated with
them, were for the most part, from my point of view, as fraudulent as the bones of St Peter, the fragments of the True Cross
and other relics revered by the pious. Then, seeing a party of
Christian pilgrims at one of these shrines, their faces bright with
faith, their voices as they sang so evidently and joyously aware
of their Saviour's nearness, I understood that for them the
shrine was authentic. Their faith made it so. Similarly, I, too,
became aware that there really had been a man, Jesus, who was
also God—I was conscious of his presence. He really had spoken
those sublime words—I heard them. He really had died on a
cross and risen from the dead. Otherwise, how was it possible
for me to meet him, as I did—in the desert wrestling with the
Devil, on that hillside preaching of how the meek inherit the
earth and the pure of heart see God, falling in step along the
road to Emmaus? As I tried to explain in my commentary (included in this volume), the words Jesus spoke are living words,
as relevant today as when they were first spoken; the light he
shone continues to shine as brightly as ever. Thus he is alive,
as for instance Socrates—who also chose to lay down his life
for truth's sake—isn't. Let the dead, as Jesus himself said, bury
their dead—in other words, relate themselves to history. Socrates is historical, the shrines and the legends are historical, the
Resurrection is historical; Jesus is alive and very truth. The
Cross is where history and life, legend and reality, time and
eternity, intersect. There, Jesus is nailed for ever to show us
how God could become a man and a man become God.

That, at least, is how I have come to see it. The old pagan gods
were all represented in terms of earthly power and wealth and

pulchritude—gleaming and mighty and lascivious. The Cross for the first time revealed God in terms of weakness and low-liness and suffering; even, humanly speaking, of absurdity. He was seen thenceforth in the image of the most timid, most gentle and most vulnerable of all living creatures—a lamb. *Agnus Dei!*—so they have been joyously singing through the centuries. *Agnus Dei!*

Through the accident of television all this, which would nor-mally be a private matter even, in contemporary terms, a private eccentricity or folly—has in some degree taken place in public, and been the subject of public comment. Every so often I get asked whether it is true that I have been received into the Roman Catholic Church. It is very difficult for me to explain that the more enchanted I become with the person and teach-ing of Christ the farther away I feel from all institutional Christianity—especially this particular institution, which, as I consider, is now racing at breakneck speed to reproduce all the follies and fatuities of Protestantism, and will surely before long arrive at the same plight, with crazed clergy, empty churches and total doctrinal confusion. Clerical criticism, one way and another, has been pretty withering; the Archbishop of York took me to task for daring to suggest that there might be Christian objections to Dr Christian Barnard's heart transplant experiments, and the Roman Catholic chaplain of Edinburgh University rebuked me for suggesting that the free distribution of contraceptives to students was conducive to sexual promis-cuity. 'The plain fact is,' the Revd. Fr. wrote, 'that we do not find elderly journalists with a gift of invective useful allies in presenting Christian standards.'

Secular criticism has been more predictable. Old friends shake their heads, and speak of me with kindly compassion, as they would if I had been run in for indecent exposure in Hyde Park; old enemies dwell on the obscenity of ageing lechers who lash out resentfully at sensual pleasures which they can no longer enjoy. My successor as Rector of Edinburgh University felici-tously described me as a 'crazed flagellant'; Peter Cook—some-one I like very much—more tolerantly contented himself with just saying I was mad. The commonest opinion is that with advancing years I have gone soft and became a bore—two perfectly plausible judgments; a more implausible one is that I have succumbed to the lures of the Establishment. Would it were so, and I had been endlessly rejecting offers of life peerages, O.B.E.s, honorary degrees and invitations to dine with the Fellows of All Souls. Alas, far from it; I have to disclose that since I began to try to be a Christian and endlessly talk about it, the chilliness with which I have long been regarded in Estabishment circles—the full range, from Lord Ritchie-Calder to Lord Thomson of Fleet—has turned into a positive ice age.

I have also received a very large number of letters, many of them of quite overwhelming sweetness and charity. I venture to quote from one which I opened as I was writing these words. The writer is a monk who had done me the high honour of reading some words of mine, which, he was kind enough to say in his letter, 'the gentle Saviour used to give me a better understanding and appreciation of our Christian heritage, and a more fervent determination to stand loyal come what may.' He goes on:

'Every morning at 5 a.m. before I go to offer the Holy Sacrifice, as a small token of my gratitude to you, I ask our beloved Saviour to be good to you and to those dear to you. I will continue to do that for whatever short time remains before I meet Him face to face.'

No one human being could possibly do another a more precious favour than this; such gestures flood the whole universe with light. I have put all these letters—some thousands of them —in a large metal box in the hope that after I am dead someone may go through them. They reveal, I think more fully than any public opinion poll or other so-called scientific investigation, the extraordinary spiritual hunger which prevails today among all classes and conditions of people, from the most illiterate to the most educated, from the most lowly to the most eminent. The various moral and theological and sociological disputes of the day, however progressively resolved with ecclesiastical connivance, have nothing to say to this spiritual hunger, which is not assuaged by legalised abortion and homosexuality, solaced by contraception, or relieved by majority rule. Nor will it take comfort in the thought that God is dead, or that mankind has come of age, or even in ecumenical negotiations for writing off Papal Infallibility against the validity of Anglican Orders. The only means of satisfying it remains that bread of life which Jesus offered, with the promise that those who ate of it should never hunger again. The promise stands.

To many of the writers of these letters it seems obvious that my life has dramatically altered its direction of recent years. This, in fact, is not so. For me the course has been from the beginning, and will be, I am sure, till the end, a series of hazards, stumblings, wrong turnings and false destinations, as it was for Bunyan's Pilgrim—which is perhaps why I love this book so dearly. Again like the Pilgrim, on picking myself up, the impulse has always been to hurry on, with some notion, however indistinct, that at last one will see the Holy City set on a hill. I have never felt much inclination to linger—not even in Vanity Fair with a view to raising the school age, extending the franchise to teenagers, nationalising the banks and otherwise improving conditions there. In the Valley of Humiliation—that green valley which is also beautified with lilies, with a very fruitful soil which doth bring forth by handfuls—'some also have wished that the next way to their father's house were here, that they might be troubled no more with either hills or mountains to go over; but the way is the way, and there's an end.' Yes, the way is the way.

Perhaps the silliest criticism of the way Jesus told us to live— and for that very reason, no doubt, the one most frequently voiced—is that it amounts to a kind of escapism, an evasion of the ardours and responsibilities of reality. Nothing could be farther from the truth. Let me give an example. The time is April 1945; the place is the East German village of Schönberg. In the little schoolhouse there is a party of prisoners, among them a Lutheran pastor, Dietrich Bonhoeffer. It is a Sunday morning, and the others press him to conduct a service. Most of the prisoners are Roman Catholics, and one of them—a Russian named Kokorin—is a Communist, but when Bonhoeffer mentions this they all with one accord press him to proceed, which he does. Ecumenicalism indeed! He takes as his text 'With his stripes we are healed, (Isaiah 53:5) and 'Blessed be the God and Father of our Lord Jesus Christ, which according to his abundant mercy hath begotten us again unto a lively hope by the resurrection of Jesus Christ from the dead.' (I Peter 1:3). An English prisoner who was present (Payne Best) has recalled how Bonhoeffer found 'just the right words to express the spirit of our imprisonment, and the thoughts and resolutions which it had brought.' Together with Bonhoeffer, all looked forward hopefully into the future.

I find this scene (for an account of which, incidentally, I am indebted to Mary Bosanquet's excellent study of Bonhoeffer—a spiritual experience in itself) infinitely touching. As the service concludes the door is flung open, and two men, standing in the doorway, tell prisoner Bonhoeffer to take his things and come with them. Before leaving he sends via Payne Best a message to his friend Dr Bell, the Bishop of Chichester—'Tell him that . . . with him I believe in the principle of our universal Christian brotherhood which rises above all national interests, and that our victory is certain.'

He is then taken to Flossenbürg where he is given the death sentence. After it has been delivered the prison doctor catches a glimpse of him through the half opened door of one of the huts, still in his prison clothes, and kneeling in fervent prayer to the Lord his God. 'The devotion and evident conviction of being heard that I saw in the prayer of this intensely captivating man', the doctor was subsequently to recall, 'moved me to the depths.' The next morning, naked under the scaffold in the sweet spring woods, Bonhoeffer kneels for the last time to pray. Five minutes later his life is ended.

As this happens, five years of the monstrous buffooneries of war are drawing to a close. Hitler's Reich that was to last for a thousand years will soon reach its ignominious and ruinous end; the liberators are moving in from the east and the west with bombs and tanks and guns and cigarettes and Spam; the air is thick with rhetoric and cant. Looking back now after twenty-four years, I ask myself where in that murky darkness any light shines. Not among the Nazis, certainly, nor among the liberators, who, as we know, were to liberate no one and nothing. The rhetoric and the cant have mercifully been forgotten;

ing. The rhetoric and the cant have mercifully been forgotten; what lives on is the memory of a man who died, not on behalf of freedom or democracy or a steadily rising Gross National Product, not for any of the twentieth century's counterfeit hopes and desires, but on behalf of a cross on which another man died two thousand years before. As on that previous occasion, on Golgotha, so amidst the rubble and desolation of 'liberated' Europe, the only victor is the man who died, as the only hope for the future lies in his triumph over death. There never can be any other victory or any other hope. This is what I am trying, so inadequately, to say.

JESUS REDISCOVERED

I was brought up to be an ardent believer in the religion of this age—utopianism. My father used to read aloud to us on Sunday evenings from books like William Morris's *Earthly Paradise*, a title which lingered in my mind as having some special significance over and above the text. I remember the scene vividly —our suburban sitting-room in South Croydon, my mother asleep in her chair, my father's voice rising and falling vigorously. He liked reading aloud; everything to do with the spoken word, especially public speaking, appealed to him. My clearest memory of him is at open-air meetings, with his words rising above the noise of traffic as he held forth about the splendid world that lay ahead when once the power of capitalism had been broken, and the public good, not private cupidity, governed and directed the works, thoughts and aspirations of mankind. I see and hear him now, a small bearded figure with broad shoulders, raised on a platform, his voice rather harsh, but penetrating; the meagre audience gathered round him, for the most part ribald or indifferent, with a few zealots in the front row. How proud I was, from my earliest years, to be one of these, exaggeratedly applauding every point he made and laughing uproariously at every joke!

To me it all seemed absolutely clear and incontrovertible. I rode in Croydon's municipal trams with a serene inward confidence that the free-enterprise buses were doomed to succumb to their challenge. I shopped for my mother in the local co-op store with a similar confidence that the lure of divi would soon capture all the business from rival, profit-making enterprises. Government secondary schools of the kind that I attended would, I was confident, provide the enlightened citizenry for our New Jerusalem when it came to pass. I joyously addressed envelopes and distributed leaflets and posters when my father was standing as a Labour candidate for the local borough council; I rang door-bells, and explained to the often irate housewife who answered that a vote for him was a vote for a better world—I did not say for paradise, but that was what I meant. I listened avidly and ecstatically when, on Saturday evenings, my father and his cronies discussed how this better world was to be brought to pass. They were mostly City clerks like himself, belonging to the lower middle class, who had moved from the Chapel with its remote expectation of a heavenly sequel to a virtuous life, into the bright glare of Fabian and Socialist certainties that tomorrow or the day after heaven could be made to exist on earth. It sometimes happened that, as I listened, I dozed or fell asleep, to be brusquely awakened and sent to bed. Their ardent words mingled with my private dreams, so that if I muttered in my sleep, more likely than not, it would be about the public ownership of the means of production, or the nationalisation of the railways and the banks.

At the same time I had a sense, sometimes enormously vivid, that I was a stranger in a strange land; a visitor, not a native. My first conscious recollection of life is of walking down the street in Sanderstead where we then lived (it must have been in about 1909, when I was six) in someone else's hat, and wondering who I was. Then, some thirty-five years later, at Allied Headquarters in Algiers, a colonel explained to me how the term 'displaced person' had been decided upon for all the various individuals who had already found, or would shortly find, themselves, as it were, loose in the world—without nationality, or place of residence, or even identity; only a vague awareness of being ostensibly such a person, born of such parents, at such a time, and now no one and belonging nowhere. As he went on talking—a rather heavy man, as I recall, running to stoutness, in an over-tight battle-dress with red tabs—it seemed to me that this was the sickest of sick expressions; an emanation of a sick world, which, as victory approached, came to seem sicker than ever.

Then I thought: After all, I'm a displaced person myself, and always have been one, from the beginning. The feeling, I was surprised to find, gave me a great sense of satisfaction, almost of ecstacy—I also in battle-dress, though with no red tabs; supposed to be fighting a war with someone or other about something or other (Oh, Churchill! Oh, finest hour!); engaged allegedly in liberating captive nations and laying low the oppressor (Help is on the way! and then that string of displaced national anthems!)—I, a D.P. I was reminded of the incident when I read about how Simone Weil in Portugal, visiting a very poor fishing village near Lisbon—Cascais, maybe—on the day of its patron saint, happened to watch the women going in procession to the ships, carrying candles and chanting 'what must certainly be very ancient hymns of a heart-rending sadness.' There, the certainty suddenly came to her 'that Christianity is pre-eminently the religion of slaves, that slaves cannot help adhering to it, and I among the others.' I cannot pretend that I had a similar certainty that Christianity is pre-eminently for D.P.s, and therefore for me. None the less, my awareness of being a D.P. made me feel uplifted in that desolate Headquarters and in the company of that ungainly colonel. Subsequently, I was to learn that You are to be found in the lowest, darkest depths, and that all who find You are thereby transported to the loftiest, brightest heights.

This sense of being a stranger, which first came to me at the very beginning of my life, I have never quite lost, however engulfed I might be, at particular times and in particular circumstances, in the pursuits of this world—whether through cupidity, vanity or sensuality; three chains which bind us, three goads which drive us, three iron gates which isolate us in the tiny, dark dungeon of our ego. For me there has always been—and I count it the greatest of all blessings—a window never finally blacked out, a light never finally extinguished. Days or weeks or months might pass. Would it never return—the lostness? I strain my ears to hear it, like distant music; my eyes to see it, a very bright light very far away. Has it gone for ever? And then—ah! the relief. Like slipping away from a sleeping embrace, silently shutting a door behind one, tiptoeing off in the grey light of dawn—a stranger again. The only ultimate disaster that can befall us, I have come to realise, is to feel ourselves to be at home here on earth. As long as we are aliens we cannot forget our true homeland, which is that other kingdom You proclaimed.

Though the religion of my home and childhood was so completely secular, I had a notion of You and a feeling about the Bible—so much so that in some weird superstitious way I would put it under my pillow at night opened at certain places. How I came to do this I have no idea, and I cannot now remember what the places were, though I think one of them may have been the thirteenth chapter of I Corinthians. I have always been bad at sleeping, and as a child—indeed, well into manhood—I was subject to nightmares. Perhaps the Bible under my pillow was intended to be some sort of protection when the night got into my head. The nightmares, incidentally, were nearly always the same—I was imprisoned in a dark place, and felt a frenzied desire to get out into the light. Once, so dreaming, I actually put my arm through the glass of my bedroom window to get out, and awoke with blood gushing out of a cut vein. I have the scar still.

My notion of You was the conventional non-sectarian one of the time—a superlatively good man, gentle and unworldly, who was done to death by the sort of people who voted Conservative and became aldermen or Justices of the Peace. If You were not actually a paid-up member of the Labour Party, it was only because there didn't happen to be a Labour Party in Galilee when You lived there. By driving the money-changers out of the temple You clearly showed that You were against capitalism; if the money-changers had been nationalised like the Post Office, or state-registered like a betting-shop, they would doubtless have been unobjectionable. My picture of You—derived, I should suppose, from popular prints like Holman Hunt's 'The Light of the World'—was long-haired, with the hair parted in the middle, bearded and wearing a crown of thorns, the eyes long-suffering and full of love despite the wrongs that had been done You, Your clothing likewise following the style usual in Bible illustrations—a sort of long coloured tunic. Your death at the hands of the authorities seemed entirely fitting. If You came back to earth, then surely, my father and his cronies concluded with my full approbation, the same fate would befall You as before; the Archbishop of Canterbury, the Lord Chief Justice and other dignitaries would see to that.

It is curious to reflect that this concept of You as a dedicated progressive and freedom-fighter is now generally approved in most clerical, and even ecclesiastical, circles. As I have found, pointing out that You resolutely refused to attach Yourself to earthly causes like Jewish nationalism, and refrained from denouncing injustices and inequalities of the time, such as slavery, amounts almost to blasphemy today. Nothing, it seems, can save You from joining Lords Soper and MacLeod on the Labour Benches in the House of Lords. Nor is it any use quoting Your own words about the tribulations and illusory hopes of this world; the new translations of the Gospels and Epistles provide a ready instrument for a continuous process of—to use the highly relevant Communist term—revisionism, whereby any position, from Lady Chatterley to squalling campus hipsters, can conveniently be incorporated in Your message. It was bad enough when the clergy identified themselves with the social and political status quo; now that they are ready to support any deviation from it, and champion anyone who can produce credentials, however dubious, of being down-trodden and oppressed, it is even worse. If there is one thing more unedifying than a ruling class in a position of dominance, it is a ruling class like ours on the run. They are capable of every folly and misjudgment, mistake their enemies for friends, and, of course, *vice versa*, and feel bound to go out of their way to encourage whatever and whoever seeks their destruction. In their forefront today one notes a bizarre contingent of crazed figures in purple and black cassocks.

Though I completely accepted the image of You derived from my father and his cronies, I had some sort of awareness from the very beginning that Your life was tragic in the sense that Lear's was, or Macbeth's. I understood dimly that this tragic You was to be seen as being in a quite different category from the progressive one. Your unique tragedy was to do with blood —as I had seen it, peeping in at the local slaughter-house; red and warm and terrible, and at the same time, it seemed, cleansing and sanctifying. Washed in the blood of the lamb!—somehow the phrase, probably from a revivalist hymn, had got into my head. I brooded over it and wondered about it; horrified at the notion, and yet also vaguely aware of what was signified by the Atonement—a sacrificial death, someone dying that others might live. Many years after, in Australia, I happened to be present at a sheep shearing. As the lambs looked up with their gentle frightened eyes, it quite often happened that the mechanical shears drew blood. The sight agitated me abnormally—the blood so red against wool so soft and white. Why did I feel as though I had seen it before, long ago? Why was the sight somehow familiar to me? Then my mind went back to the slaughter-house, and to being washed in the blood of the lamb. That was it—the sacrificial lamb, *Agnus Dei.*

My father would certainly have described himself as an essentially religious man. Like many early supporters of the Labour Party he had come in via the Chapel, and his mental attitudes continued to the end of his life to bear strong traces of nonconformity—in his case, Congregationalism. Even to this day the style of Labour Party oratory and official gatherings is more reminiscent of Methodism than Marxism. None the less, my father and his cronies took up an agnostic position; they liked making jokes about 'God Almighty' which were mildly shocking to my mother, who stubbornly maintained some sort of Christian orthodoxy. On one occasion she remarked to me with great emphasis, when I had been expressing doubts about the story of Daniel in the lions' den: 'If Daniel isn't true then nothing is.' I paid more heed to an observation of my father's, delivered on numerous occasions, that he disliked the cross as he did any other gibbet. This seemed to me extremely amusing, and I tried it out myself on my fellow schoolboys, though without much effect one way or the other; they were neither amused nor shocked.

Raising a laugh by being shocking was a large element in the agnosticism of early Socialists like my father. A similar technique half a century later gave the B.B.C. television programme *That Was the Week That Was,* and all its derivatives, their great appeal. Truly I have lived to see the poor jokes of my near-proletarian childhood become the wit of the reluctant bourgeoisie of my late middle-age. How often Alan Bennett, Peter Cook and the other young satirists of the fifties and sixties have carried me back to our little suburban sitting-room, and my father and his cronies holding forth about the Establishment's grotesque villainies and Anglican Christianity's fatuities! The first story I ever wrote—in printed letters when I was very young—was about a train which, to the delight of the passengers, went zooming along through station after station without stopping, until it failed to stop at their particular stations. Then they yelled and howled in protest, but it made no impression on the engine-driver, who just took the train roaring on. It was only long afterwards that I understood what the story meant.

Despite my father's ostensible agnosticism, we had quite an acquaintanceship among Anglican clergymen and dissenting ministers. These were Labour sympathisers prepared under certain circumstances to take the chair at our meetings. We were glad to have them; their presence provided a certain guarantee of respectability—or so we supposed—which in those far-off days was sorely needed. We were still liable to be charged with being believers in 'free love', the abolition of marriage and the family, and other, as they were then considered, disreputable causes. Though we indignantly denied these charges, claiming that our moral standards were decidedly higher than our accusers', some of them stuck. The Soviet regime's early ebullient attitude to marriage, divorce and abortion was used against us, and certain individuals belonging to our own flock—Dr Aveling, Marx's son-in-law, and H. G. Wells were extreme examples—were vulnerable in this respect. Closer at hand, there was the Whiteway Colony, near Stroud in Gloucestershire, started and conducted by some of my father's friends and associates, where marriage and money were both eschewed as bourgeois-capitalist abominations. I had spent some months near Whiteway in my ninth year, when I developed symptoms of tuberculosis, and was ordered by the doctor to be in the country. So I knew that the colonists were given to nude bathing and other interesting but unconventional behaviour. My father went out of his way to hold them up to friendly ridicule as being more absurd than immoral, and did not allow our association with them to blunt our indignant repudiation of any propensity to preach or practise sexual promiscuity. I should suppose that my father's actual behaviour was impeccably virtuous whatever he might say about bourgeois morality. But successive Labour governments have introduced permissive legislation on matters like homosexuality, abortion and divorce, which could be taken as justifying the charges of moral turpitude made against the Labour movement in its early days. At the same time, the Soviet regime has turned into one of the few strongholds of puritanism in the mid-twentieth century. This has led to considerable confusion on the Left. If it is part of enlightenment to be tolerant of homosexuals, sexual promiscuity and marital infidelity, how can this be combined with admiring the U.S.S.R., where perversion, eroticism and divorce are looked at askance? Such complexities lay ahead. In my childhood years there seemed no possible question but that we were the true exponents of virtue, both private and public; the true heirs of the Christian tradition, even though we had thrown overboard Christian dogmas along with the Christian deity.

The clergymen and ministers who were prepared to join with us on this basis conformed to a type, rare enough then, but now prevalent, if not pretty well universal, in all denominations, with the possible exception of the Roman Catholics, though since Pope John's Ecumenical Council, multiplying rapidly among them, too. They visited us from time to time, and I can remember them well : men in black suits, pipe-smokers for the most part; a bit restless in their places, fidgety, and somehow— how can I put it?—coarse and 'physical'; their breathing heavy, their tongues very red and their lips very full, their laughter and their talk over-eager. I found them repulsive. They represented, one can now see, the beginning of a powerful tide which was to sweep through the churches, transforming exhortation into demagogy, creeds into political programmes, and transcendentalism into utopianism. All we wanted of them was that they should grace our gatherings with their cloth, and this they were prepared to do. Behind their backs, we ridiculed their compliance and gullibility, but to their faces we were polite and respectful. My own feeling about them was crystallised in Moscow in the early thirties when I had occasion to show one of them round an anti-God museum. As we moved from one exhibit to another, pausing before the books displayed long enough for their blasphemous titles to be translated, I wondered when a sense of shock or disapproval would register on his amiable countenance. It never did; with his broad expanse of clerical collar shining in the late autumn sunshine, he departed even more cheerfully than he came. In the light of this and other like experiences, I have come to regard clerical Christianity and its officers as totally farcical—as Kierkegaard puts it, a folding screen behind which the Christian evades the real strenuousness of being a Christian. Momentarily, I have to admit, with Protestant romanticism I toyed with the notion that the Roman Catholic Church, with its longer tradition, tougher discipline and more rigid doctrine, would prove an exception, and manage to resist the Gadarene slide on which the other denominations had embarked so blithely and disastrously. How mistaken I was! Already most of the Nonconformist denominations are at their last gasp, and the Church of England is sustained only by the ostensible importance that is derived from its connection with the State. It will be surprising now if the Roman Church does not find itself in a similar case in a matter of years rather than decades. No doubt the Ecumenical movement will be stimulated by this sense of corporate weakness, but it is unlikely that unity brought about on such a basis will prove either enduring or a source of additional strength—rather, if anything, the reverse.

In the no-man's-land between the churches and progressive politics there existed institutions like Brotherhoods and Socialist Sunday Schools; vaguely 'religious' in character, but eschewing transcendentalism of every kind; a sort of agnosticism sweetened by hymns. My father was a favourite speaker at Brotherhood meetings. His particular blend of political idealism and religiosity from his Chapel days was just what was wanted. In

any case he, too, rather liked speaking from a pulpit. Had he
been born some decades earlier I think he would have been a
preacher rather than a political propagandist. When, later on,
he became a Member of Parliament I was surprised to notice
how little to his taste were the stratagems and devices of
machine politics in which he was necessarily involved. He was
most at home with moral issues—a self-indulgence I have in-
herited. Of our local Socialist Sunday School I have only the
dimmest memory, and cannot have attended more than once or
twice. We sang hymns of sorts, and reverently considered the
brotherhood of man; there were readings from *News from
Nowhere* and, I think, Winwood Reade's *The Martyrdom of
Man*; we were exhorted to renounce the devil of capitalism and
all his works, and confidently await our reward in the coming
of the New Jerusalem in the shape of a Socialist Co-operative
Commonwealth. My recollection is that, apart from the absence
of any reference to a deity, the procedure was indistinguishable
from that of any other Protestant Sunday School. There was
even a collection.

The Quakers also welcomed my father as a speaker, and I
vividly remember going to a Friends' Meeting House with him.
During the period of quiet meditation, as I observed, he bowed
his head with the others; when he came to address them, it was
in quieter accents than he normally adopted. To me, the
Quakers symbolised riches; my mother would whisper to me
how wealthy they were, and it was true, as I knew, that a good
part of my father's election expenses would be contributed by
his Quaker friends and admirers. Their sober but expensive
clothes, their simple but well-appointed houses, filled me with
awe mixed with distaste. I detected, as I thought, something
worldly in their unworldliness; a kind of oatmeal sensuality in
their austerity, something greedy in their self-abnegation.

In any case, I was generally uneasy, not just about Quakers,
but about this whole concept of a Jesus of good causes. I would
catch a glimpse of a cross—not necessarily a crucifix; maybe two
pieces of wood accidentally nailed together, on a telegraph pole,
for instance—and suddenly my heart would stand still. In an
instinctive, intuitive way I understood that something more im-

portant, more tumultuous, more passionate, was at issue than our good causes, however admirable they might be. Something to do with the deep, inner nature of life itself—mine, and all life. Something inescapable, pursuing and pursued, for ever beyond my reach and yet under my hand; part of the air I breathed, and lost in the wide firmament above. As was to happen to me so often, I found in Blake the exact words:

> To see a World in a grain of sand,
> And a Heaven in a wild flower,
> Hold Infinity in the palm of your hand,
> And Eternity in an hour.

I can remember the first time my eyes rested on lines by Blake (actually, 'Ah, Sun-flower! weary of time'), and the extraordinary feeling I had of some unique distillation of understanding and joy, a unique revelation of life's very innermost meaning and significance.

I find it more difficult to recall and recount the feelings I had about the cross even before it meant anything to me as such. It was, I know, an obsessive interest; something I avidly sought out, as inflamed senses do erotica. I might fasten bits of wood together myself, or doodle it. This symbol, which was considered to be derisory in my home, was yet also the focus of inconceivable hopes and desires—like a lost love's face, pulled out and gazed at with sick longing. As I remember this, a sense of my own failure lies leadenly upon me. I should have worn it over my heart; carried it, a precious standard never to be wrested out of my hands; even though I fell, still borne aloft. It should have been my cult, my uniform, my language, my life. I shall have no excuse; I can't say I didn't know. I knew from the beginning, and turned away. The lucky thieves were crucified with their Saviour; You called me, and I didn't go those empty years, those empty words, that empty passion!

A south London suburb in the years of the 1914–18 war—which was where I spent my childhood—provided a rootless, faithless, and, I should suppose, rather sick environment. The hysteria of violence was very much in the air; military bands played the soldiers who were leaving for the front to the railway station; officers on leave caroused at the Greyhound Hotel, and women on war work exuded a randy tang which I sensed, without understanding, other than vaguely, what it signified. It was, as I now see, a manner of life which was to become general —made up of lights rather than substances, of movement rather than settlement. We schoolboys had the freedom of the streets by day and by night; the vast holocaust taking place across the Channel—sometimes vaguely heard in a distant roar of guns, or dimly seen in a silver zeppelin gliding across the sky leaving a trail of noise and fire—seemed in our eyes a stupendous spectacle in which, if only it went on long enough, there was a part for us. Greatly daring, I even, in my sixteenth year, timorously went into a recruiting office to volunteer, but withdrew in confusion when asked for a birth certificate. If, outwardly, out of reverence for my father, I shared his sombre mood when he scanned the long casualty lists, and echoed his hopes that the projected League of Nations would make this war one to end war and usher in a better, juster world, inside me I only longed that peace might be delayed until I, too, had donned a uniform like my older brothers, seen men die, and found a hero's comfort and recompense in the arms of lovely women.

Such unrealised hopes lingered on until, some two decades later, they seemed about to be belatedly realised; but by then, I was already middle-aged; any available lovely women were likewise well past their springtime, and the new war, in any case proved to be a non-war as far as we were concerned— fought elsewhere, by other arms than ours; a conflict outside our provenance, opera-bouffe whose comic captains and seedy kings were most reluctant to depart. The other, earlier war, regrettably from my point of view, duly ended. From the open top of a bus threading its way laboriously through the teeming streets, I watched the scenes of celebration. It was the first time I had seen what human beings are like when they cast aside all restraint—shouting, grimacing, flushed, extravagant in their jubilation. The scene with its apocalyptic flavour recalled to me vividly the lurid Doré illustrations in an edition of Dante's *Inferno* among my father's books whose pages I often turned over.

Religious instruction, so called, at first my elementary, and then my secondary school, consisted of Bible stories and secular moral tales, suspended in favour of mental arithmetic when examinations or government inspectors loomed. I maintained an attitude of detached contempt, as befitted the son of a Socialist and agnostic, and enjoyed airing my view that the Bible was demonstrably untrue, and the moral tales a mean device to keep the downtrodden and oppressed content with their lot. At morning prayers the headmaster often made us repeat 'Hallowed be Thy name' three or four times to get the aspirate right—which on one occasion induced me, in fear and trembling, but with outward bravado, to raise my hand in class afterwards and ask whether it was considered that the deity was as particular about sounding our aitches as the headmaster. The smile of the teacher and the giggles of my classmates made me feel pleased with myself, but even then my satisfaction was touched with a nagging worry that I had been in some incomprehensible way cheap and disloyal—to what or to whom I had no idea. The same sort of experience has befallen me again and again. On how many mornings have I, like Peter, heard the cock crow thrice with an aching heart! Even in those far-off days most of the elementary and secondary school teachers would have called themselves free-thinkers, and were already assiduously preparing the way for the climate of prevailing agnosticism today. A future social historian is likely to decide that the most powerful instrument of all in bringing about the erosion of our civilisation was none other than the public education system set up with such high hopes and at so great expense precisely to sustain it.

Through a school friend I got into the way of occasionally attending the services in a Congregational chapel near my home. It was a grey stone building in neo-gothic style with a tall steeple. The minister, a man from the Hebrides with a long white beard, seemed to me a prophetic figure, but my true motive for attending his services was to look at girls—something a good deal less easily attainable then than it is today. As I devoutly bent my head in prayer I would peer through my fingers at a girl's head similarly bent, brooding on her unresponsiveness to my passion, perhaps even unawareness of it; on her female body, warm and hidden, under her clothes. The officers' uniforms in the congregation—there would always be one or two at least who were home on leave—inevitably put an amorous schoolboy in the shade; after the service, lurking noisily and hopefully in the street outside, I was left to make my way home alone. Of the service itself I remember little except the hearty hymns and tremulously ardent voice of the bearded minister. Even then it was a dying cult; already the life was draining out of it—those heavy wooden pews emptying, the pulpit words losing whatever fire they still had, likewise the reading from the majestic Bible on its brass rest. Fewer and fewer would, as the years passed, remain in their places to swallow the little cubes of bread and sip the unfermented wine of the Last Supper.

The tide of the twentieth century was flowing in a different direction altogether. It was the picture palaces, their fronts so brilliantly lighted, inside so mysteriously dark, that provided our true churches and chapels. There we sat, separately or clasped together, in scented darkness (in those days attendants during intervals squirted perfume like Flit over the heads of the patrons in their seats) and worshipped our tribal gods—sex, money and violence—as they were projected on to the screen and entered into our own minds and bodies. Thus the new gospel was propounded—in the beginning was the Flesh and the Flesh became Word; to be carnally minded is life—dying in the Spirit to be re-born in the Flesh. There was no more ardent acolyte than I, and yet, trudging homewards late at night along the empty tram-lines, a fearful sense of desolation would fall upon me. I strained my ear, but heard only the sound of my own footsteps; I peered ahead, but saw nothing except the tramlines reaching into the distance. And You—where were You then? Ready! the answer comes back—ready, but unsummoned.

In 1920, when I was seventeen, I went to Cambridge, rather, as it seems in retrospect, in fulfilment of my father's aspirations than of mine. It was he, not I, who spoke of an Alma Mater, of sporting one's oak, etc., etc. His Fabian heroes, in their tweed suits and ample coloured ties, with their enriched voices and flow of eager words, seemed to him the flower of mankind, and he hoped that Cambridge would make me another such. Alas, dear man, it was not to be. His innocent snobbishness, of a kind very prevalent in the Labour Party, then as now, led him, without his being aware of it, to want to have me made in the image of all that, as a Socialist, he most deplored. I thought of this years later when Lord Snow, after a spirited recommendation of comprehensive schools to his fellow-peers, let out that he was sending his own son to Eton. Only as children of God are we equal; all other claims to equality—social, economic, racial, intellectual, sexual—only serve in practice to intensify inequality. For this reason Your commandment to love our fellow men follows after, and depends upon, the commandment to love God. How marvellous is the love thus attained—the faces looming up, young and old, sullen and gay, beautiful and plain, clever and stupid, black, pink and grey; all brothers and sisters, all equally dear!

My college (Selwyn) was full of ordinands, most of them ex-service; in my youthful eyes, ravaged and wild-looking, wearing British warms and ready, at the drop of a hat, to launch off into a blood-curdling account of slaughter on the Western Front or in Gallipoli. They were perhaps—and who shall blame them?—a little bit mad, and their Christian faith correspondingly somehow crazed. I believe that with many of them it all wore off, and they either abandoned the idea of the Church, or settled down to be run-of-the-mill clergymen. At the time, however, they were full of wild fancies of leading a crusade which would re-convert post-war England—nickname men, after Woodbine Willie or Tubby Clayton, who saw themselves as combining the attributes of saint and demagogue, marching in a cassock at the head of a great procession winding its way to the New Jerusalem. Their dream, too, was to be realised belatedly in the person of Canon Collins and the C.N.D. movement.

Chapel in those days was compulsory, and I became familiar with the order of Anglican services and the Book of Common Prayer, almost the only beneficial result of the four years I spent at Cambridge. There was also a great deal of other religious activity in the shape of meetings and discussions and retreats. I remember particularly Father Vernon, an Anglican monk from

Stanford-le-Hope where I spent a few days with him. He was a dark, impressive, ardent man who for a short while enjoyed a considerable vogue, and then, as I vaguely learnt, became a Roman Catholic and was heard of no more. With a vague notion of joining his order, I awaited some vision or guidance which never came, and in the end departed with relief, conscious, as I thought, of something inadequate, even phoney, about the place. Was it flight or dismissal; pursued or pursuing—or both? In this quest for You we look without finding and find without looking. And to the very end—like Bunyan's Pilgrim who, with Mount Sion and the Heavenly Hosts actually in view, and but one river still to cross, stumbled, and dreaded that the water would close over his head. But for Hopeful's reassuring words he might have fallen even there.

At Cambridge the afterglow of the Oxford Movement was still discernible. Most of the ordinands I knew were, to a greater or lesser degree, Anglo-Catholics, and had heroic tales to tell of introducing the Reserved Sacrament in the teeth of a congregation's opposition; of vestments, up to and including lace, despitefully worn, and incense despitefully wafted (like that perfume in the picture palaces) over worshippers' heads. I remember being taken to breakfast with a certain Father Tooth, a venerable figure who had once been stoned for conducting services in what was considered to be a Romish style; the offending vestment and the actual stone thrown being mounted in a glass case and available for inspection. This martyrdom failed to impress me. Preoccupation with ritual has always seemed to me comparable, in matters of worship, with preoccupation with erotic techniques in matters of sex. Bearing out the comparison, the literature on the subject reads very like the *Kama Sutra*. I got in the way, at this time, of partaking at the early morning Communion service; took the wafer into my mouth and drank from the cup, expecting rare nourishment from this spiritual food, crossing myself and bowing down accordingly. You never came to me in Your body and Your blood, dispensed as the Blessed Elements by an intoning priest. Very different from Stanford-le-Hope was the Oratory House at Cambridge where I resided for several terms as a result of my friendship with A.V.—a friendship which has lasted now for the best part of half a century, growing ever more delightful and comfortable—he being a member of this brotherhood of Anglican priests. We said the offices through the day, and in the afternoons I usually worked in the garden under the direction of Wilfred Knox, brother of Ronnie, one of those enchanting human beings who seem to have no more than half a foot in this world. It was altogether a rather idyllic existence as I recall it; I'm sure You were there, in the little chapel and in the garden, but somehow I missed You. Truly, one needs eyes to see. How easily I understand how even Mary could mistake You for the gardener! As I look back I realise that the only times I have been happy have been in simplicity and austerity; a little white room with a chair and a table, fruit and rice on a green leaf, a barrack hut or a tent—such circumstances bring their own ecstasy, and You within reach, or at any rate hailing distance. What insanity, then, to bury one's head in the trough; to glut the senses and inflate the ego to monstrous proportions, thereby ensuring that You are inexorably lost to view! That extraordinary lostness that overwhelms one, flesh against flesh, gorging, or avidly looking up where the remorseless arc lights beat down! So the years have gone, and only a remnant of life remains, which still You may deign to accept, as I dare hope.

Otherwise, Cambridge, so far as I was concerned, consisted of boredom, dissatisfaction, and misty afternoon walks. Ever after, the notion of higher education as a panacea for contemporary ills has seemed to me a total absurdity—more than ever so today. From Cambridge I went to Alwaye in South India to join the staff of the Union Christian College there. The College was on the top of a remote hill by the Periyar River, and had only just been started by a dedicated band of Indian Christians. I grew to love them and the place; when I went back some forty years later everything seemed just the same, except that I had grown old, and most of those I knew there were dead—the same austere hostels in one of which I had lived, the same stony hill-side which I had so often climbed up and down, the same swift-flowing river in which I had so often bathed, the same students moving silently, bare-footed, in their white shirts and *dhoties*. Thinking then about it, I realised that in the company of these good and dedicated men I was given my last chance to enlist definitively in Your service, but that I turned away. All the circumstances were perfect—the remoteness, so that even the British Raj scarcely impinged on us; the fellowship and true austerity; and You. Yes, You were there, I know—which, I suppose, was why I had to go. However far and fast I've run, still over my shoulder I'd catch a glimpse of You on the horizon, and then run faster and farther than ever, thinking triumphantly: Now I have escaped. But no, there You were, coming after me. Very well, I'd decide, if I can't get away by running, I'll shut my eyes and ears and not see or hear You. No good! one sees and hears You, not with the eyes and ears, but inwardly, with the soul, whose faculties never can be quite put out however gorged, stupefied and ego-inflated we may become. Now I can flee no farther; I fall. Mercy!

The years that followed were spent almost wholly in the wilderness of this world where the profession of journalism permits one to be a sort of power-voyeur, peering through key-holes at the antics of the great, and deriving therefrom little spasms of obscene excitement. Even so, however enraptured I became, I could never shake off the feeling that the spectacle was Theatre rather than Life—entries and exits, words spoken, postures adopted, all previously rehearsed, with a prompter handy to help the players with their lines. The times are out of sync, I'd often say to myself, (especially in the House of Commons Press Gallery), noting how some outpouring of rhetoric bore no relation to the drama currently being played, but belonged to another on which the curtain had long ago fallen and the audience departed; likewise the make-up, the lighting, the costumes, the scenery, so that the players, coming on to the stage, stumbled, bumping into cardboard walls and groves which, according to the script they were following, should not have been there. I, too, played my little accompanying jig on a typewriter keyboard—'The people of this country will never for a moment countenance ...' 'Our two great countries will ever march forward together ...' 'British policy is, and must ever be, based on fidelity to . . .' When I peer into the past I hear all these dead words whistling through its cavernous emptiness. How wise You were to decline the Devil's offer of the kingdoms of the earth! The offer, as You well understood, was fraudulent; there are no kingdoms—only script-writers, make-up girls, a wardrobe-mistress, a stage manager. As for that other kingdom, Yours, which is not of this world—it alone is real. The cross is real wood, the nails are real iron, the vinegar truly tastes bitter and the cry of desolation is live, not recorded.

Your aphorism about rendering unto Caesar the things that are Caesar's deprives power of its sting. (What a brilliant aphorism, by the way; quite in the vein of Machiavelli, whose attitude to power is so infinitely preferable to, say, a Woodrow Wilson's, Gilbert Murray's or an Eleanor Roosevelt's, and has done so much less harm!) Sensual appetites are disposed of less easily. When the Devil makes his offer (always open incidentally) of the kingdoms of the earth, it is the bordellos which glow so alluringly to most of us, not the banks and the counting-houses and the Snow-swept corridors of power. We can easily resist becoming millionaires, privy-councillors or chairmen of the Prices and Incomes Board, but to swim away on a tide of sensual ecstasy, to be lost in another body, to fly as high as the ceiling on the wings of the night, or even of the afternoon—that, surely, is something. The imagination recoils from the prizes, or toys, of a materialist society. Who but some half-witted oil sheik or popular actor can go on desiring sleek yachts or motor-cars or white villas perched above yellow sands? But what about the toys in living flesh? The Barbie dolls that bleed? The Hefner playmates that move? The celluloid loves for ever panting and for ever young?

Sex is the mysticism of a materialist society, with its own mysteries—this is my birth pill; swallow it in remembrance of me!—and its own sacred texts and scriptures—the erotica which fall like black atomic rain on the just and unjust alike, drenching us, blinding us, stupefying us. To be carnally minded is life! So we have ventured on, Little Flowers of D. H. Lawrence; our Aphrodites rising, bikini'd and oiled, from Côte d'Azur beaches; drive-in Lotharios, Romeos of the motorways, glow-

B

ing and burning like electric log fires, until—cut!—the switch is turned off, leaving the desolate, impenetrable night. Did I sometimes, staring sleepless into it, even then catch a glimpse, far, far away, of a remote shading of the black into grey? A minuscule intimation of a dawn that would break? You!

It was padding about the streets of Moscow that the other dream—the kingdom of heaven on earth—dissolved for me, never to be revived. Those grey anonymous figures, likewise padding about the streets, seemed infinitely remote, withdrawn, for ever strangers, yet somehow near and dear. The grey streets were paradise, the eyeless buildings the many mansions of which heaven is composed. I caught another glimpse of paradise in Berlin after it had been liberated—there the mansions made of rubble, and the heavenly hosts, the glow of liberation still upon them, bartering cigarettes for tins of Spam, and love for both. (Later, this paradise was transformed by means of mirrors into a shining, glowing one, running with *schlag* and fat cigars, with bartered love still plentifully available, but for paper money, not Spam.) So many paradises springing up all over the place, all with many mansions, mansions of light and love; the most majestic of all, the master-paradise on which all the others were based—on Manhattan Island! Oh, what marvellous mansions there, reaching into the sky! What heavenly *Muzak* overflowing the streets and buildings, what brilliant lights spelling out what delectable hopes and desires, what heavenly hosts pursuing what happiness on magic screens in living colour!

And You? I never caught even a glimpse of you in any paradise—unless You were an old coloured shoe-shine man on a windy corner in Chicago one February morning, smiling from ear to ear; or a little man with a lame leg in the Immigration Department in New York, whose smiling patience as he listened to one Puerto Rican after another seemed to reach from there to eternity. Oh, and whoever painted the front of the little church in the woods at Kliasma near Moscow—painted it in blues as bright as the sky and whites that outshone the snow? That might have been You. Or again at Kiev, at an Easter service when the collectivisation famine was in full swing, and

Bernard Shaw and newspaper correspondents were telling the world of the bursting granaries and apple-cheeked dairy-maids in the Ukraine. What a congregation that was, packed in tight, squeezed together like sardines! I myself was pressed against a stone pillar, and scarcely able to breathe. Not that I wanted to particularly. So many grey, hungry faces, all luminous, like an El Greco painting; and all singing. How they sang—about how there was no help except in You, nowhere to turn except to You; nothing, nothing, that could possibly bring any comfort except You. I could have touched You then, You were so near—not up at the altar, of course, where the bearded priests, crowned and bowing and chanting, swung their censers—One of the grey faces, the greyest and most luminous of all.

It was strange in a way that I should thus have found myself nearest to You in the land where for half a century past the practice of the Christian religion has been most ruthlessly suppressed; where the very printing of the Gospels is forbidden, and You are derided by all the organs of an all-powerful State as once you were by the Roman soldiers when they decked you out as a ribald King of the Jews. Yet on reflection, not so strange. How infinitely preferable it is to be abhorred, rather than embraced, by those in authority. Where the distinction between God and Caesar is so abundantly clear, no one in his senses—or out of them, for that matter—is likely to suggest that any good purpose would be served by arranging a dialogue between the two of them. In the Communist countries an unmistakable and unbridgable abyss divides the kingdoms of the earth and Your kingdom, with no crazed clerics gibbering and grimacing in the intervening no-man's-land. It provides the perfect circumstances for the Christian faith to bloom anew—so uncannily like the circumstances in which it first bloomed at the beginning of the Christian era. I look eastwards, not westwards, for a new Star of Bethlehem.

It would be comforting to be able to say: Now I see! To recite with total satisfaction one of the Church's venerable creeds—'I believe in God, the Father Almighty....' To point to such a moment of illumination when all became miraculously clear. To join with full identification in one of the varieties of

Christian worship. Above all, to feel able to say to You: 'Lord!' and confidently await Your command. Comforting—but alas, it would not be true. The one thing above all others that You require of us is, surely, the truth. I have to confess, then, that I see only fitfully, believe no creed wholly, have had no all-sufficing moment of illumination.

And You—what do I know of You? A living presence in the world; the one who, of all the billions and billions and billions of our human family came most immediately from God and went most immediately to God, while remaining most humanly and intimately here among us, today, as yesterday and tomorrow; for all time. Did You live and die and rise from the dead as they say? Who knows, or for that matter, cares? History is for the dead, and You are alive. Similarly, all those churches raised and maintained in Your name, from the tiniest, weirdest conventicle to the great cathedrals rising so sublimely into the sky—they are for the dead, and must themselves die; are, indeed, dying fast. They belong to time, You to eternity. At the intersection of time and eternity—nailed there—You confront us; a perpetual reminder that, living, we die and, dying, we live. An incarnation wonderful to contemplate; the light of the world, indeed.

Fiat lux! Let there be light! So everything began at God's majestic command; so it might have continued till the end of time—history unending—except that You intervened, shining another light into the innermost recesses of the human will, where the ego reigns and reaches out in tentacles of dark desire. Having seen this other light, I turn to it, striving and growing towards it as plants do towards the sun. The light of love, abolishing the darkness of hate; the light of peace, abolishing the darkness of strife and confusion; the light of life, abolishing the darkness of death; the light of creativity, abolishing the darkness of destruction. Though, in terms of history, the darkness falls, blacking out us and our world, You have overcome history. You came as light into the world, that whoever believed in You should not remain in darkness. The promise stands for ever. Your light shines in the darkness, and the darkness has not overcome it. Nor ever will.

AM I A CHRISTIAN?

This is a question I mull over from time to time without finding a satisfactory or convincing answer. If I put it to myself after, say, reading one of the Archbishop of Canterbury's pronouncements in the House of Lords on contemporary *mores* or listening to some radio or television evangelist of Beveridgeanity, I feel profoundly thankful not to be, even in name, associated with such as they. If they are Christian, I reflect, then I emphatically am not. On the other hand books like *Resurrection* or *The Brothers Karamazov* give me an almost overpowering sense of how uniquely marvellous a Christian way of looking at life is, and a passionate desire to share it. Likewise, listening to Bach, reading Pascal, looking at Chartres Cathedral or any of the other masterpieces of Christian art and thought. As for the Gospels and Epistles, I find them (especially St John) irresistibly wonderful as they reduce the jostling egos of now—my own among them—to the feeble crackling flicker of burning sticks against a majestic noonday sun. Is it not extraordinary to the point of being a miracle, that so loose and ill-constructed a narrative in an antique translation of a dubious text should after so many centuries still have power to quell and dominate a restless, opinionated, over-exercised and under-nourished twentieth-century mind?

I am well aware, of course, that just to be thus quelled and dominated is far from amounting to being a Christian. In any case, what is a Christian today? One may well ask. From the days when the Very Revd. Hewlett Johnson used to expatiate in Canterbury Cathedral upon the Christian excellence of the late Stalin, to even loftier heights of psychedelic piety, there is scarcely a contemporary absurdity which has not received some degree of clerical, if not episcopal, endorsement. Rebellious or randy fathers come to the microphone to tell us of the doubts which

have assailed them and of the hazards of priestly celibacy;
learned theologians bend their powerful minds to demonstrat-
ing that God is dead and his Church, therefore, becomes a useless excrescence. Holy discothèques, sanctified playmates,
Bishop Pike of California—dear God! how well I remember
him—Bishop ('call me Jim') Pike, and his memorable observation as we made our way arm in arm to the hospitality room
from the B.B.C. television studio where we had been doing our
little stint of Soper opera. St Paul, he said, was wrong about
sex. So he was, Bishop, so he was!

One may marvel that, when pretty well every item of Christian belief and of Christian ethics has been thus subjected to
some degree of denigration and attack by those ostensibly
responsible for upholding and propagating them, congregations
of sorts none the less continue to assemble in parish churches on
Sunday mornings, and ordinands and novices, though in
dwindling numbers, continue to come forward with seemingly
authentic vocations. The Church of Christ has to stagger on
under the guidance of those who increasingly sympathise with,
when they do not actually countenance, every attack on its doctrines, integrity and traditional practices. By one of our time's
larger ironies, ecumenicalism is triumphant just when there is
nothing to be ecumenical about; the various religious bodies are
likely to find it easy to join together only because, believing
little, they correspondingly differ about little. I look forward to
the day when an Anglican bishop in full canonicals will attend a
humanist rally on the South Downs, or a Salvation Army band
lead a procession of Young Atheists to lay a wreath on Karl
Marx's grave in Highgate Cemetery. It cannot be long delayed,
if it has not happened already.

It would take a subtle ear indeed to catch out of all this
confusion any consistent or coherent theme. Institutional Christianity, it seems to me, is now in total disarray, and visibly
decomposing, to the point that, short of a miracle, it can never
be put together again with any semblance of order or credibility.
In their present state of decomposition the various Christian
denominations are not even an impediment to Christian belief
but just a joke. One notes the grimaces of sacerdotal faces as,

holding their noses, they try to swallow *Humanae Vitae*; the bizarre convolutions of Quakers when they venture out on the nursery-slopes of sex, with the same sort of wry satisfaction as one does the tergiversations of an Anglican bishop who recently undertook baptising a new Polaris submarine, or, for that matter, the tread of the sometime nuclear marchers through the division lobby in support of the Government which decreed its construction.

Yet curiously enough the very intensity of all this confusion, the very preposterousness of the effort to market dust and ashes as body-building, and a kingdom not of this world as profitable real estate, somehow for me clears the air for a consideration of what Christianity really is about. The surrender of institutional Christianity to the promoters of a kingdom of heaven on earth has been so abject, the assumptions of scientific materialism are so widely accepted and arrogantly stated, that an aspiring Christian today is left in a kind of catacomb of his own making, utterly remote from the debates and discussions going on around him, whether about 'permissive' morality (divorce, contraception and abortion—those three panaceas for all matrimonial ills), or about the basic dogma of the Christian faith.

In my copy of the New Testament I underline passages which take my fancy. Nearly all of them are about the deceitfulness of the cares of this world and of riches, about how concupiscence and vanity separate us from God, about glorying in tribulation which brings patience, experience and hope, about the flesh lusting against the spirit and the spirit against the flesh, these being contrary to one another so that we cannot do the things that we would do, and so on. It is difficult to think of any sentiments which would be more intrinsically unsympathetic in most clerical circles. They are, I should say, about the most unpopular sentences it is possible to utter today; at religious gatherings they cause malaise and irritation; on radio and television panels derision and incredulity. When I use them I am often accused of insincerity or affectation, so rooted are the opposite assumptions—that by caring about this world we shall make it better, that we must aim collectively to get richer in order to get happier and happier, that the unrestrained satisfaction of our earthly hopes and desires is the way to physical, mental and spiritual contentment.

However, I love these sentences, and often say them over to myself. I should like them to govern my every thought and activity for the rest of my life. They seem to me to be true, and the notion of making the world better by caring about it, and achieving happiness through material prosperity and sensual pleasure, quite nonsensical. In face of the otherworldliness which I still unfashionably find in the Gospels, as far as I am concerned the whole edifice of twentieth-century materialism—and the utopian hopes that go therewith—falls flat on its face. One is delivered from the myth of progress. The terrible vision of a Scandinavian–American paradise, with longer lives, more and better aphrodisiacs and more leisure and amenities for all, dissolves into nightmare, awaking from which one advances gingerly upon the sublime truth that to live it is necessary to die, that a life can only be kept by being lost—propositions which strike contemporary minds as pessimistic, but which seem to me optimistic to the point of insanity, implying as they do, that it is possible for mere man, with his brief life and stunted vision, to aspire after a universal understanding and a universal love. Is this being a Christian? Ask me another.

New Statesman, 10 March 1967

IS THERE A GOD?

Well, is there? I myself should be very happy to answer with an emphatic negative. Temperamentally, it would suit me well enough to settle for what this world offers, and to write off as wishful thinking, or just the self-importance of the human species, any notion of a divine purpose and a divinity to entertain and execute it. The earth's sounds and smells and colours are very sweet; human love brings golden hours; the mind at work earns delight. I have never wanted a God, or feared a God, or felt under any necessity to invent one. Unfortunately, I am driven to the conclusion that God wants me.

God comes padding after me like a Hound of Heaven. His shadow falls over all my little picnics in the sunshine, chilling the air; draining the viands of their flavour, talk of its sparkle, desire of its zest. God takes a hand as history's compère, turning it into a soap opera, with ham actors, threadbare lines, tawdry props and faded costumes, and a plot which might have been written by Ted Willis himself. God arranges the lighting —Spark of Sparks—so that all the ravages of time, like parched skin, decaying teeth and rotting flesh, show through the make-up, however lavishly it may be plastered on. Under God's eye, tiny hoarded glories a little fame, some money ... *Oh Mr M! how wonderful you are!*—fall into dust. In the innermost recesses of vanity one is discovered, as in the last sanctuaries of appetite; on the highest hill of complacency, as in the lowest burrow of despair. One shivers as the divine beast of prey gets ready for the final spring; as the shadow lengthens, reducing to infinite triviality all mortal hopes and desires.

There is no escape. Even so, one twists and turns. Perhaps Nietzsche was right when he said that God had died. Progressive theologians with German names seem to think so : *Time* magazine turned over one of its precious covers to the notion. If God were dead, and eternity had stopped, what a blessed relief to one and all! Then we could set about making a happy world in our own way—happy in the woods like Mellors and his Lady Chatterley; happiness successfully pursued, along with life and liberty, in accordance with the Philadelphia specification; happy the Wilson way, with only one book to take to the post-office—one book, one happiness; happy in the prospect of that great Red Apocalypse when the State has withered away, and the proletariat reigns for ever more. If only God were D. H. Lawrence, or Franklin D. Roosevelt, or Harold Wilson, or Karl Marx!

Alas, dead or alive, he is still God, and eternity ticks on even though all the clocks have stopped. I agree with Kierkegaard that 'what man naturally loves is finitude' and that involvement through God in infinitude 'kills in him, in the most painful way, everything in which he really finds his life . . . shows him his own wretchedness, keeps him in sleepless unrest, whereas finitude lulls him into enjoyment.' Man, in other words, needs protection against God as tenants do against Rachmanism, or minors against hard liquor.

Where is such protection to be found?

One of the most effective defensive systems against God's incursions has hitherto been organised religion. The various churches have provided a refuge for fugitives from God—his voice drowned in the chanting, his smell lost in the incense, his purpose obscured and confused in creeds, dogmas, dissertations and other priestly pronunciamentos. In vast cathedrals, as in little conventicles, or just wrapped in Quaker silence, one could get away from God. Plainsong held him at bay, as did revivalist eloquence, hearty hymns and intoned prayers. Confronted with that chanting, moaning, gurgling voice—'Dearly beloved brethren, I pray and beseech you . . .' or with that earnest, open, Oxfam face, shining like the morning sun with all the glories flesh is heir to, God could be relied on to make off.

Unfortunately, this defensive system has now proved to be a Maginot Line, easily by-passed by hordes of happiness-pursuers, some in clerical collars and even mitres, joyously bearing a cornucopia of affluence, and scattering along their way birth pills, purple hearts and other goodies—a mighty throng whose trampling feet clear a path as wide as a motorway, along which God can come storming in.

Another defence against God has been utopianism, and the revolutionary fervour that goes therewith. A passion to change the world and make it nearer to the heart's desire automatically excludes God, who represents the principle of changelessness, and confronts each heart's desire with its own nullity. It was confidently believed that a kingdom of heaven on earth could be established, with 'God, Keep Out' notices prominently displayed at the off-limits. In practice, the various versions of this kingdom have one and all proved a failure; utopian hopes washed away in the blood of Stalin's purges, reduced to the dimensions of Mr Wilson's one book, liberated out of existence.

Few any longer believe in the coming to pass of a perfect, or even a Great, society. There never was a less revolutionary climate than now prevails, when almost any *status quo*, however ramshackle, can stand—Tito's, Franco's, Ulbricht's. Why, tourism today is a more dynamic force than revolution, swaying, as it does, crowns and thrones; Thomas Cook and the American Express, not the *Internationale*, unite the human race. In Africa, it is true, regimes still totter and fall, but even there the wind of change blows as it listeth. Even when the great day comes, and the white bully-boys are dispossessed to be replaced by black ones, it will be history, not progress, that has spoken.

With the Church no longer a sanctuary, and utopianism extinguished, the fugitive from God has nowhere to turn. Even if, as a last resort, he falls back on stupefying his senses with alcohol or drugs or sex, the relief is but short-lived. Either he will sink without trace for ever into that slough, or, emerging, have to face the inescapable confrontation. It is a fearful thing to fall into the hands of the living God—thus Kierkegaard (and also Cromwell) groaned in desperation.

What living God? A being with whom one has a relationship, on the one hand, inconceivably more personal than the most intimate human one, to the point that, as we are told, God has actually counted the hairs of each head; on the other, so remote that in order to establish a valid relationship at all, it is necessary to die, to murder one's own flesh with the utmost ferocity, and batter down one's ego as one might a deadly snake, a cobra which has lifted its hooded head with darting forked tongue, to sting. (I say 'a being' which suggests a person, a spirit, a genie coming out of a bottle, and so is utterly inappropriate. There are no adequate words for any of the great absolutes, like life and death, good and evil; only for trivialities like politics and economics and science. One falls back on the meaningless monosyllable, God, as Hindu *sadhus* in their spiritual exercises endlessly repeat the equally meaningless monosyllable, Oom.)

What can be said with certainty is that, once the confrontation has been experienced—the rocky summit climbed, the interminable desert crossed—an unimaginably delectable vista presents itself, so vast, so luminous, so enchanting, that the small ecstasies of human love, and the small satisfactions of human achievement, by comparison pale into insignificance. Out of tactical despair comes an overwhelming strategic happiness, enfolded in which one is made aware that every aspect of the universe, from a tiny grain of sand to the light-years which measure its immeasurable dimensions, from the minutest single living cell to the most complex human organism, are ultimately related, all deserving of reverence and respect; all shining, like glow-worms, with an intrinsic light, and, at the same time, caught in an all-encompassing radiance, like dust in a sunbeam.

This sense of oneness, with the consequent release from the burden of self, I take to be God—something which indubitably exists; which not only has not died, but cannot die. Such has been the testimony of those in the past whom I most revere— like Christ, St Paul, St Augustine and St Francis, Pascal, Bunyan, Blake, Tolstoy and Dostoevsky. To their testimony, with the greatest possible diffidence, I add my own, so hesitant, fitful and inarticulate.

New Statesman, 6 May 1966

THE CRUCIFIXION

One thing at least can be said with certainty about the Crucifixion of Christ; it was manifestly the most famous death in history. No other death has aroused one hundredth part of the interest, or been remembered with one hundredth part of the intensity and concern.

Practically every European artist, great and small, has planned or executed a representation of it, from the Italian primitives to Francis Bacon. Most writers, likewise, have made use of the scene and its imagery in their work, if only for the purposes of ridicule or blasphemy. *Nouvelle vague* film-makers, and Hollywood impresarios in search of a sure-fire box-office success, equally turn to it for a theme. Walking recently with Graham Sutherland in hills overlooking the Mediterranean I found he was always on the look-out for thorns, as though they were precious jewels—as indeed they are for him, ever since he painted the crown on Christ's stricken head.

The cross, symbol of this macabre execution, has been carried pretty well everywhere, within and outside Christendom. No corner of the world is so remote and inaccessible that you may not find a cross there.

As for Europe, in countries like Italy and France it is impossible to go a hundred yards anywhere without being confronted with some version or other of the Crucifixion. Since that Golgotha happening, billions have been made, from exquisitely fashioned ones to the most tawdry, gimcrack, mass-produced ones; from huge overpowering Calvarys to little tiny jewelled crucifixes to hang round the neck or over the heart, but always with the same essential characteristics—a man at the last extremity of a cruel death, with lolling head, and feet and hands viciously nailed to a wooden cross.

In theory such a symbol should be depressing. It portrays the defeat of goodness by duplicity and power; a meek and broken victim of the kind of human brutality to which we, perhaps more than most generations of men, have had to accustom ourselves. In practice the symbol has inspired some of the gayest figures in history, like St Francis of Assisi; has filled the cities of Renaissance Italy with a profusion of art which has been the admiration of Christian and non-Christian alike; and has stimulated audacities of thought and exploration which have carried the human race forward with immense strides towards understanding and mastering their material circumstances.

How unlikely anything of the kind would have seemed at the time! Who among the motley collection of spectators of so obscure an event could possibly have envisaged that there before their eyes another civilisation was being born which would last for two thousand years, shining so long and so brightly. Not even the Apostles could have thought of that; what they looked for was an apocalyptic Second Coming and the end of the world, not the beginning of Christendom. Only St Paul, converted *after* the Crucifixion from a persecutor of Christians to one of Christ's most ardent and brilliant followers, may have vaguely sensed something of the kind. I nourish a secret hope in my heart, as our civilisation decomposes into People's Hedonism, with, not one, but whole armies of crazed Neros sucking LSD sugar and babbling protest songs, that another obscure Crucifixion may have taken place that will in due course lighten the darkness now falling so thick and so fast. If so, we should not know; it would not get on to the telly or into the newspapers.

A believing or orthodox Christian would, of course, account for the durability of the cross's appeal over the centuries by the divinity of the man crucified. God, he would say, was put to death by unredeemed men, and then rose from the dead; naturally, so unique and definitive an event has continued, and ever will continue, to hold the attention of mankind.

I have to confess that to me—as I should suppose, to the great majority of present-day inheritors of the Christian tradition— such a line of thought is largely meaningless. With the utmost difficulty, and in the vaguest possible manner, I can grasp some sort of notion of a deity, and of his loving purpose, in which I, in common with all creation, am inextricably enmeshed. I can even, in moments of illumination, imagine myself to be in contact with such a deity, and surrender myself with inexpressible happiness to his will. To imagine this deity having a son in any particular sense, and this son to have been born of a virgin, and to have lived on earth for thirty years or so as a man; then to have died and to have risen from the dead, is, as far as I am concerned, beyond credibility.

I quite agree that we of the twentieth century are perfectly capable of believing other things intrinsically as improbable as Christ's incarnation. Towards any kind of scientific mumbo-jumbo we display a credulity which must be the envy of African witch-doctors. While we shy away with contumely from the account of the creation in the Book of Genesis, we are probably ready to assent to any rigmarole by a Professor Hoyle about how matter came to be, provided it is dished up in the requisite jargon and associated, however obliquely, with what we conceive to be 'facts'.

I suppose every age has its own particular fantasy. Ours is science. A seventeenth-century man like Pascal, though himself a mathematician and scientist of genius, found it quite ridiculous that anyone should suppose that rational processes could lead to any ultimate conclusions about life, but easily accepted the authority of the Scriptures. With us it is the other way round.

What, then, does the Crucifixion signify in an age like ours? I see it in the first place as a sublime mockery of all earthly authority and power. The crown of thorns, the purple robe, the ironical title 'King of the Jews,' were intended to mock or parody Christ's pretensions to be the Messiah; in fact, they rather hold up to ridicule and contempt all crowns, all robes, all kings that ever were. It was a sick joke that back-fired. No one it seems to me, who has fully grasped the Crucifixion can ever again take seriously any expression or instrument of worldly power, however venerable, glittering or seemingly formidable.

When Christ was tempted in the wilderness he declined the Devil's offer to give him sway over the kingdoms of the earth (a refusal which must be intensely irritating to those who believe that it is possible through Christian good-will to set up a kingdom of heaven on earth); the Crucifixion demonstrated why—because the Devil's offer was bogus. There are no kingdoms for him to bestow; only pseudo or notional ones presided over by mountebanks masquerading as emperors and kings and governments.

Look under the crown and you see the thorns beneath; pull aside the purple robe, and lo! nakedness; look into the grandiloquent titles and they are seen to be no more substantial than Christ's ribald one of King of the Jews scrawled above his cross. In Christ's day the Roman emperors claimed to be gods and induced their subjects to pay them divine honours. He, a man, exposed the hollowness of their claim by dying, thereby becoming God in the eyes of successive generations of men, who went on worshipping him long after the Roman Empire had ceased to exist.

In this sense, Christ's death on the cross may be seen as the exact converse of the next most famous death as far as our civilisation is concerned—that of Socrates. Socrates obediently drank hemlock and died to support and enhance the State: Christ died on the cross in derisive defiance of all States, whether Roman, Judaic, or any other.

From Socrates' death emanate all plans for the collective betterment of mankind, whether embodied in a nation, a regime, a leader, an ideology, a social system, or, for that matter, a Church; from the cross, the notion of individual salvation, of individual souls journeying through life like Bunyan's Pilgrim, all equal in their capacity as children of God and in that Christ died for them equally, and all buoyed up by the expectation of deliverance through death from the demands and imperfections of their fleshly existence.

What, I often ask myself, was the Golgotha happening actually like. Clearly, in no wise as momentous in the eyes of those who witnessed it as the retrospective attention lavished upon it would seem to imply. Upon history at the time it made absolutely no impact. To understand this one has to think of an administratively comparable incident in times past in one of the remoter parts of the then extant British Empire—for instance, the execution in Burma that Orwell attended when he was a young police officer there, and afterwards described so feelingly and perceptively.

I well remember the good-naturedly contemptuous attitude in the days of the Raj of the British soldiery in India to Hindu and Muslim religious fanaticism. The Roman soldiers in Palestine, I expect, took a similar attitude towards Jewish religious fana-ticism. I doubt if Christ made any particular impression on them; in their eyes he was just another wog to be crucified. One imagines the conversation in the sergeants' mess that night, with some old hand pointing out to a slightly squeamish new-comer lately arrived from Rome that with the Jews you have to be firm and stand-offish; give 'em an inch and they take an ell—I heard it all word for word in up-country clubs in India forty years ago.

For some reason I always see in my mind's eye a fringe of Roman troops ringing the little crowd round the cross, and standing out against the Golgotha skyline in their breast-plates and togas—not very high-grade troops either, in that distant unpopular station. They look on nonchalantly, their orders are not to interfere, but to make sure that if there's any trouble it doesn't spread. An N.C.O. is in charge; the officers are away at the games, or maybe Their Excellencies, the Pilates, are giving a garden party to celebrate the Emperor's birthday.

As for the indigenous spectators (as they are described in the official report which Pilate gets the next day, and barely glances at), they consist of a few sharp-eyed, bearded rabbis making sure that everything goes according to plan, the usual sightseers attracted by executions, street-accidents or any other violence; some of the disciples, including Peter, still, poor fellow, full of contrition about his denial of Christ the day before (who hasn't similarly heard the cock crow, alas?), Mary and one or two other women, and maybe a representative of the underground Jewish resistance movement just in case something cropped up, though not with much hope.

Christ's remark about rendering unto Caesar the things that are Caesar's effectively eliminated any momentary expectation that he might espouse the cause of liberating the Jews from their servitude to Rome. As it turned out, Palestine was to be liberated on numerous occasions in the course of a rather tragic history, but never by him.

It was the sort of incident—a man dying in that slow public way—which must have generated its own immediate tension in the beholders, even though they were unaware of the nature and magnitude of the stupendous drama being enacted before them. In some vague way they expect something to happen, and so it does; the man expires, not with a gesture of defiance befitting a putative King of the Jews, but with a cry of despair. With that cry Christendom comes to pass. We are henceforth to worship defeat, not victory; failure, not success; surrender, not defiance; deprivation, not satiety; weakness, not strength. We are to lose our lives in order to keep them; to die in order to live.

It is true, of course, that professing Christians and ostensibly Christian societies and institutions have by no means been true to the cross and what it signified, especially today when the nominally Christian part of the world is foremost in worship of the Gross National Product—our Golden Calf—and in pursuit of happiness in the guise of sensual pleasure. Yet there the cross still is, propounding its unmistakable denunciation of this world and of the things of this world.

There had to be a sequel; I quite see that. The man on the cross who had given up the ghost must rise from the dead as a living God; the Resurrection followed the Crucifixion as inevitably as day follows night. And, indeed, in a sense it clearly happened. Otherwise, how should I, a twentieth-century nihilist, who asks nothing better than to live out his days without any concern for a God, living or dead, be worrying his head about this cross and a man who died on it two thousand years ago? Whether it happened as described in the Gospel narrative, and endlessly repeated by Christian apologists, is another question. In any case, what does it matter?

I even prefer to suppose that some body-snatcher, accustomed to hanging about Golgotha to pick up anything that might be going, heard in his dim-witted way that the King of the Jews was up for execution. Good! he thinks: there are bound to be pickings there. So he waits till the job is done, finds out where the corpse has been laid, drags the stone away and then, making sure no one is watching, decamps with the body.

What a disappointment for him! This King of the Jews has no crown, no jewels, no orbs, no sceptre, no ring; he is just a worthless, wasted, broken, naked body. The man contemptuously abandons the body to the vultures, who in their turn leave the bones to whiten in the sun—those precious, precious bones!

Observer, 26 March 1967

CREDO

In trying to formulate what I believe I have to begin with what I disbelieve. I disbelieve in progress, the pursuit of happiness and all the concomitant notions and projects for creating a society in which human beings find ever greater contentment by being given in ever greater abundance the means to satisfy their material and bodily hopes and desires. In other words, I consider that the way of life in urbanised, rich countries, as it exists today, and as it is likely to go on developing, is probably the most degraded and unillumined ever to come to pass on earth. The half-century in which I have been consciously alive seems to me to have been quite exceptionally destructive, murderous and brutal. More people have been killed and terrorised, more driven from their homes and native places; more of the past's heritage has been destroyed, more lies propagated and base persuasion engaged in, with less compensatory achievement in art, literature and imaginative understanding, than in any comparable period of history.

Ever since I can remember, the image of earthly power, whether in the guise of schoolmaster, mayor, judge, prime minister, monarch or any other, has seemed to me derisory. I was enchanted when I first read in the *Pensées* (Pascal being one of the small, sublime band of fellow-humans to whom one may turn and say in the deepest humility: 'I agree') about how magistrates and rulers had to be garbed in their ridiculous ceremonial robes, crowns and diadems. Otherwise, who would not see through their threadbare prentensions? I am conscious of having been ruled by buffoons, taught by idiots, preached at by hypocrites and preyed upon by charlatans in the guise of advertisers and other professional persuaders, as well as by verbose demagogues and ideologues of many opinions, all false.

Nor, as far as I am concerned, is there any recompense in the so-called achievements of science. It is true that in my lifetime more progress has been made in unravelling the composition and mechanism of the material universe than previously in the whole of recorded time. This does not at all excite my mind, or even my curiosity. The atom has been split; the universe has been discovered, and will soon be explored. Neither achievement has any bearing on what alone interests me—why life exists, and what is the significance, if any, of my minute and so-transitory part in it. All the world in a grain of sand; all the universe too. If I could understand a grain of sand I should understand everything. Why, then, should going to the moon and Mars, or spending a holiday along the Milky Way, be expected to advance me farther in my quest than going to Manchester and Liverpool, or spending a holiday in Brighton?

Education, the great mumbo-jumbo and fraud of the age, purports to equip us to live, and is prescribed as a universal remedy for everything, from juvenile delinquency to premature senility. For the most part, it only serves to enlarge stupidity, inflate conceit, enhance credulity and put those subjected to it, at the mercy of brain-washers with printing presses, radio and television at their disposal. I have seen pictures of huge, ungainly, prehistoric monsters who developed such a weight of protective shell that they sank under its burden and became extinct. Our civilisation likewise is sinking under the burden of its own wealth, and the necessity to consume it; of its own happiness, and the necessity to provide and sustain the fantasies which embody it; of its own security, and the ever more fabulously destructive nuclear devices considered essential to it. Thus burdened, it, too, may well soon become extinct. As this fact sinks into the collective consciousness, the resort to drugs, dreams, fantasies and other escapist devices, particularly sex, becomes ever more marked.

Living thus in the twilight of a spent civilisation, amidst its ludicrous and frightening shadows, what is there to believe? Curiously enough, these twilit circumstances provide a setting in which, as it seems to me, the purpose which lies behind them stands out with particular clarity. As human love only shines in all its splendour when the last tiny glimmer of desire has been extinguished, so we have to make the world a wilderness to find God in it. The meaning of the universe lies beyond history, as love lies beyond desire. That meaning shines forth in moments of illumination (which come and go so unaccountably; though, I am thankful to say, never quite ceasing—a sound as of music, far, far away, and drowned by other more tumultuous noises, but still to be faintly and fitfully heard) with an inconceivable clarity and luminosity. It breaks like a crystalline dawn out of darkness, and the deeper the darkness the more crystalline the dawn.

Let me express it, as I have often thought of it, in terms of a stage. In the middle is the workday world where we live our daily lives, earning a living, reading newspapers, exchanging money, recording votes, chattering and eating and desiring. I call this the Café Limbo. On the left of the stage is an area of darkness within which shapes and movements can be faintly discerned, and inconclusive noises heard; sounds and sweet airs which, as on Caliban's island, give delight and hurt not. I call this Life. The right of the stage is bright with arc-lamps like a television studio. This is where history is unfolded and news is made; this is where we live our public, collective lives, seat and unseat rulers, declare wars and negotiate peace, glow with patriotism and get carried away with revolutionary zeal, enact laws, declaim rhetoric, swear eternal passion and sink into abysses of desolation. I call this the Legend.

Across this triple stage, between Life, the Café Limbo and the Legend, a drama is endlessly presented. Two forces shape the play—the Imagination which belongs to Life, and the Will which belongs to the Legend. Out of the Imagination comes love, understanding, goodness, self-abnegation; every true synthesis ever grasped or to be grasped. Out of the Will comes lust, hatred, cupidity, adulation, power, oratory; every false antithesis ever propounded or to be propounded. Those who belong exclusively or predominantly to Life are saints, mystics and artists. In extreme cases—Christ, for instance—they have to be killed. (This is superbly explained in the famous Grand In- quisitor passage in *The Brothers Karamazov*, Dostoevsky be- ing, like Pascal, of the small sublime band.) Those who belong exclusively or predominantly to the Legend are power-maniacs, rulers, heroes, demagogues and liberators. In extreme cases—Hitler, for instance—they bring about their own destruction. In Life there is suffering, deprivation and sanity; in the Legend, happiness, abundance and madness.

Most of us spend the greater part of our time in the Café Limbo, casting an occasional glance in the direction of Life, and more than an occasional one in the direction of the Legend. Laughter is our best recourse, with the bar to provide a fillip as and when required. The Café Limbo is licensed. When a character passes from the Legend into Life he brings some of the light with him; shining like a glow-worm, until gradually the light subsides and goes out, swallowed up in the darkness of Life.

This same pattern may be traced more particularly and tragically in a single countenance, as anyone will be aware who has had occasion to watch over a loved face hovering between sanity and madness. (And many have; for as we abolish the ills and pains of the flesh we multiply those of the mind. By the time men are finally delivered from disease and decay all pasteurised, their genes counted and rearranged, fitted with new, replaceable, plastic organs, able to eat, copulate and perform other physical functions innocuously and hygienically as and when desired—they will all be mad, and the world one huge psychiatric ward.) You study the loved, distracted face as a scholar might study some ancient manuscript, looking for a key to its incomprehensibility. What you see is a fight to the death between the Will and the Imagination. If the former wins, then the flickering light will be put out for ever; if the latter, it will shine again, to burn with a steady radiance, and you can cry out from a full heart: 'Oh, beloved, you have come back to me.'

I am well aware that, psychiatrically speaking, this is nonsensical. Yet I believe it. I see these two forces struggling for mastery in each individual soul; in mine, in all men's; in each collectivity, throughout our earth and throughout the immeasurable universe. One is of darkness and one of light; one wants to drag us down into the dark trough to rut and gorge there, and the other to raise us up into the azure sky, beyond appetite, where love is all-embracing, all-encompassing, and the dark confusion of life sorts itself out, like an orderly, smiling countryside suddenly glimpsed from a high hill as the mists disperse in the sun's light and warmth. One is the Devil and the other God. I have known both, and I believe in both.

For us Western Europeans, the Christian religion has expressed this ancient, and, as I consider, obvious dichotomy in terms of breath-taking simplicity and sublimity. It was not the first word on the subject, nor will it be the last; but it is still *our* word. I accept it. I believe, as is written in the New Testament, that if we would save our lives we must lose them; that we cannot live by bread alone; that we must die in the flesh to be reborn in the spirit, and that the flesh lusts contrary to the spirit and the spirit contrary to the flesh; that God cannot see a sparrow fall to the ground without concern, and has counted the hairs of each head, so that all that lives deserves our respect and reverence, and no one man can conceivably be more important, of greater significance, or in any way more deserving of consideration than any other. God is our father, we are his children, and so one family, brothers and sisters together.

It is true that these basic propositions of Christianity have got cluttered up with dogma of various kinds which I find often incomprehensible, irrelevant and even repugnant. All the same, I should be proud and happy to be able to call myself a Christian; to dare to measure myself against that sublimely high standard of human values and human behaviour. In this I take comfort from another saying of Pascal, thrown out like a lifeline to all sceptical minds throughout the ages—that whoever looks for God has found him.

At its most obscurantist and debased, the Christian position still seems to me preferable to any scientific–materialist one, however cogent and enlightened. The evangelist with his lurid tract, calling upon me to repent for the Day of Judgment is at hand, is a burning and shining light compared with the eugenist who claims the right to decide in his broiler-house mind which lives should be protracted and which must be put out; or with the colporteurs of sterility who so complacently and self-righteously display their assortment of contraceptives to the so-called 'backward' peoples of the world as our civilisation's noblest achievement and most precious gift.

The absurdities of the kingdom of heaven, as conceived in the minds of simple believers, are obvious enough—pearly gates, angelic choirs, golden crowns and shining raiment. But what are we to think of the sheer imbecility of the kingdom of heaven on earth, as envisaged and recommended by the most authoritative and powerful voices of our time? Wealth increasing for evermore, and its beneficiaries, rich in hire-purchase, stupefied with the telly and with sex, comprehensively educated, told by Professor Hoyle how the world began and by Bertrand Russell how it will end; venturing forth on the broad highways, three lanes a side, with lay-bys to rest in and birth pills to keep them *intacta*, if not *virgo*, blood spattering the tarmac as an extra thrill; heaven lying about them in the supermarket, the rainbow ending in the nearest bingo hall, leisure burgeoning out in multitudinous shining aerials rising like dreaming spires into the sky; happiness in as many colours as there are pills—green and yellow and blue and red and shining white; many mansions, mansions of light and chromium, climbing ever upwards. This kingdom, surely, can only be for posterity an unending source of wry derision—always assuming there is to be any posterity. The backdrop, after all, is the mushroom cloud; as the Gadarene herd frisk and frolic they draw ever nearer to the cliff's precipitous edge.

I recognise, of course, that this statement of belief is partly governed by the circumstance that I am old, and in at most a decade or so will be dead. In earlier years I should doubtless have expressed things differently. Now the prospect of death overshadows all others. I am like a man on a sea voyage nearing his destination. When I embarked I worried about having a cabin with a porthole, whether I should be asked to sit at the captain's table, who were the more attractive and important passengers. All such considerations become pointless when I shall so soon be disembarking.

As I do not believe that earthly life can bring any lasting satisfaction, the prospect of death holds no terrors. Those saints who pronounced themselves in love with death displayed, I consider, the best of sense; not a Freudian death-wish. The world that I shall soon be leaving seems more than ever beautiful; especially its remoter parts, grass and trees and sea and rivers and little streams and sloping hills, where the image of eternity is more clearly stamped than among streets and houses. Those I love I can love even more, since I have nothing to ask of them but their love; the passion to accumulate possessions, or to be noticed and important, is too evidently absurd to be any longer entertained.

A sense of how extraordinarily happy I have been, and of enormous gratitude to my creator, overwhelms me often. I believe with a passionate, unshakable conviction that in all circumstances and at all times life is a blessed gift; that the spirit which animates it is one of love, not hate or indifference, of light, not darkness, of creativity, not destruction, of order, not chaos; that, since all life—men, creatures, plants, as well as insensate matter—and all that is known about it, now and henceforth, have been benevolently, not malevolently, conceived, when the eyes see no more and the mind thinks no more, and this hand now writing is inert, whatever lies beyond will similarly be benevolently, not malevolently or indifferently, conceived. If it is nothing, then for nothingness I offer thanks; if another mode of existence, with this old worn-out husk of a body left behind, like a butterfly extricating itself from its chrysalis, and this floundering muddled mind, now at best seeing through a glass darkly, given a longer range and a new precision, then for that likewise I offer thanks.

Observer, 26 June 1966

A HARD BED TO LIE ON

Nothing, I suppose, could be more alien to the spirit of this age than monasticism. Just for that reason, it has always had a particular fascination for me. The quiet, the order, the essential simplicity of a monk's way of life, all seemed alluring in a world increasingly given over to noise, violence and the avid pursuit of what passes for happiness. My own life, I should in honesty add, has been far from monkish, and it is only latterly that the positive aspects of monasticism, as distinct from just turning away from one's own vomit, have become comprehensible to me.

An opportunity to pursue this interest further arose when the B.B.C. asked me to take part in the filming of an enclosed religious order for a television programme. This involved spending three weeks in a Cistercian abbey—at Nunraw in Scotland. It might be supposed that it would be impossible for an outsider to get to know Cistercians, who follow the strict Trappist rule of silence. In fact the rule as now applied does not preclude necessary conversation. The monks no longer need to practise their weird sign-language, and anyway they were given a special dispensation to speak to me. I have rarely been thrown with such talkative and agreeable men. I grew very fond of them, and think of them still with the utmost affection.

My first acquaintance with them, however, was rather forbidding. I went up to Nunraw some months before the filming began, to explain the project, first to the Abbot, and then to the assembled community. They were gathered in an assembly hall which, as I subsequently discovered, they use for their chapters: their faces seemed very remote, almost forbidding, as I looked anxiously around at them. Their identical costume (nowadays priests and lay-brothers wear the same habit) and cropped heads added to the sombre effect.

I could not but recall prison audiences to whom I have occasionally given lectures. The difference was that, whereas prisoners' faces mostly look brutalised and angry, or just withdrawn into a sullen vacuity, the monks' faces, as I noted on closer examination, were serene; some of them, as it seemed to me, actually shining with inward sanctity. Goodness, of course, does shine, whereas evil casts a physical, as well as moral, shadow where it falls. At the Transfiguration the disciples present were positively dazzled by the shining ecstasy in Christ's face; when poor Judas picked up his thirty pieces of silver a cold and terrible gloom, I am sure, hung like a cloud over the scene.

I explained to the monks that I had always been interested in monasticism and hoped it would prove possible to show on the television screen what life in an enclosed order like theirs was really like: also to provide an explanation out of their own mouths of what induced them to forgo things like marriage, pleasure, success, money; all that in a materialist society like ours is considered to make life worth living.

The commonest judgment to be heard in the outside world, I said, was that they were fugitives from reality rather than seekers after a reality of their own. They were thought of as selfish, cowardly men who sought the attainment of their own serenity by cutting themselves off from the conflicts and dilemmas which afflicted their fellows. Preoccupied exclusively with their own salvation, they left the world to its fate.

They listened to me, as I thought, stonily. Most of them, remember, had never seen television or read a secular newspaper (thereby incomparably blessed, as I continually pointed out to them) and knew nothing of me apart from chance references, by no means always complimentary, in the Catholic publications they were permitted. Their questions, when they came to put them, were sharp and to the point. How did they know that my presentation of them would be truthful and not slanted? Did it make sense for monks whose vocations had led them into an enclosed order to parade themselves before millions of viewers? What assurance had they that differing points of view among them about the role of monasticism in the twentieth century would find just expression? I should add that the voices of the older monks had a decided sepulchral timbre, no doubt due to the strict following over years of their rule of silence; the younger ones who joined the order when the rule had already been relaxed spoke more normally.

I did my best to answer their questions adequately, and would seem to have succeeded in satisfying them. The Abbot told me subsequently that doubts were set at rest and approval given to our project. I was interested to learn that the monks' approval, as distinct from the Abbot's, was required before we could proceed. Contrary to the commonly held view, a Cistercian community is a highly democratic organisation; the Abbot is elected, and important policy decisions are taken by a majority vote of all the monks.

Having agreed to co-operate, the monks could not have been more helpful, and took a suprisingly realistic view of the exigencies of filming. For instance, it was necessary to ask them when they were being filmed working in the fields, to wear their habits instead of denims as they normally do, because otherwise viewers might think they were farm-workers employed by the monks. They got the point at once, and agreed to a mild deception which in the ordinary way would have been unpalatable. I found in them a curious combination of realism and other-worldliness. On reflection I decided that it is only the other-worldly who know how to cope with this world; St Francis, I'm sure, was much more practical than, say, Lord Beeching, as Simone Weil (to me the one true saint and mystic of our time) much preferred Machiavelli to Franklin D. Roosevelt. So, by the way, do I.

I stayed in the abbey and tried as far as possible to share the monks' way of life. Perhaps I hoped thereby to experience some marvellous illumination; in any case, it seemed the best way to catch the spirit of the place. I was called at 4 a.m. for Mass at 4.30; the monks had risen an hour before for their first prayers and meditations. The very early morning has always appealed to me greatly; even after a debauch, or a night of being blitzed (individual and collective versions of the same folly), I remember the enchantment of the half-light and stillness before the noise of day begins again.

In the chapel—a converted army hut of 1914–18 vintage—the monks were already praying; immobile, white, shadowy figures, until the lights were put up and Mass began, jointly celebrated by all the priests in the community. To me it meant nothing, apart from the pleasant sound of plainsong and my efforts to follow the Latin. The essential notion of eating Christ's flesh and drinking his blood is something I neither understand nor appreciate.

After Mass I went for a walk on the moors above the abbey. It was the lambing season, and as I looked at the young lambs frisking about, words I had just heard—*Agnus Dei*—echoed in my mind. What a terrific moment in history that was, I reflected, when men first saw their God in the likeness of the weakest, mildest and most defenceless of all living creatures!

Nearby was the new abbey, which the monks set about building soon after they came to Nunraw from their parent house in Roscrea, Tipperary, in 1946. It is nearly finished now; an elegant, well-constructed building whose design is based on the abbey at Citeaux in Burgundy, where their order was founded in 1098. The monks hope to move into it before long from their present temporary quarters in a rather ugly, inconvenient Neo-Gothic mansion supplemented by army hutments. In planning their new abbey a community of a hundred was anticipated; as things have turned out, they are barely half that number.

Vocations are scarce today, especially in the enclosed orders, and present indications are that they will get scarcer. Some of the monks, too, take the view that the new abbey is too lavishly designed, and consider that the money spent on it might have been better devoted to feeding the hungry. I was glad, I told them, that such a view had not prevailed when Chartres Cathedral was being built.

The monks, including the Abbot, all live in dormitories without even the privacy of a cell. I should find this a hard deprivation. Father Benedict, the guest-master, provided me with the luxury of a guest-room to myself, and looked after me with loving care. When I thanked him he said that St Benedict had laid it down that all guests should be treated as though they were Christ. This rule, as I had every reason to know, he punctiliously observed. I had my meals by myself, but with approximately the same diet as the monks; they subsist on cheese, vegetables, fruit, bread, butter and milk, but I had an occasional egg as well. Cheese is a fairly recent addition to their diet, and in the old days their food was carefully measured out. Now they take as much as they want. They eat in their refectory in total silence, with one of the monks reading aloud to them from a devotional work.

After breakfast and an office most of the monks went off to the fields to work. Their farming, as far as I could judge, is fairly up-to-date, but they decided (rightly, I'm sure) to eschew broiler-house and factory-farm methods. How is it possible to look for God and sing his praises while insulting and degrading his creatures? If, as I had thought, all lambs are the *Agnus Dei*, then to deprive them of light and the fields and their joyous frisking and the sky is the worst kind of blasphemy. The monks, at any rate, find such practices repellent. Some of them, however, are doubtful about farming as a means of supporting themselves, and wonder whether it might not be more satisfactory to work in some outside industrial enterprise. Here, too, I pointed out, they would run into difficulties, as the worker-priests had found.

The young student-monks, or 'scholastics' as they are called, spend their mornings in study. Their chief instructor is Father Ambrose (the Father Zossima of the community, I decided) who takes them through Thomas Aquinas with great verve and, I am sure, erudition. He is one of the shining ones; after talking with him, one finds oneself uplifted, walking on air, not so much for anything he has said, but just from his presence.

Father Ambrose's instruction, though regarded with the utmost respect, does not satisfy the scholastics. They have somehow imbibed many of the nonsensical notions of the age; *Honest to God* has, as it were, got into the woodwork. Their seclusion at least gives them a bit of leeway; ten years hence, I expect, they will have got round to Ginsberg, Marshall McLuhan, Jagger and Laing, God help them. We had many disputes

in the course of which I found myself ardently denouncing the
world to young monks as ardently concerned to uphold it—a
decidedly bizarre reversal of roles, which, as far as I was concerned, only endeared them to me the more.

Among the monks, the old guard who came over with the
Abbot from Roscrea stood out as Irish to the backbone, priests
and lay-brothers alike. The Abbot himself is a remarkable man;
tiny in stature, full of energy, shrewdness, humour and a true
sanctity. I had many conversations with him and learnt much
from him about monasticism as seen through the eyes, not of an
exalté, but of one of God's henchmen. Then there are the lay-
brothers like Brother Oliver, who directs the farming. White-
haired, sharp-eyed and ruddy-complexioned, his piety is of the
earthy kind, but none the poorer for that. His family circumstances in Tipperary, he told me, required him to choose between marriage and religion, and he chose the latter. He has
never regretted his choice. As he nears his end he looks forward
with a simple, cheerful expectation to going to heaven; the just
reward for the ardours of his Cistercian life.

Among those who have joined the community since the
migration to Nunraw there are several Anglican converts in
whose eyes one may still occasionally catch a glint of the Thirty-
nine Articles; also numerous local artisans like Brother Andrew,
a skilled electrician from John Brown's shipyard, who worked
on the *Queen Mary*. One notices him at once; a little bent man
with a white Walt Disneyish beard. He told me that he had
started by trying to preach to his shipyard mates, and then he
decided it would be more satisfactory to pray for them. This is
what he has been doing ever since. When he had finished
speaking with me before the cameras I thanked him for the
perfect simplicity and shining truthfulness of what he had said.
He replied that it had not been him speaking at all.

As I got to know the monks, they soon belied my original
impression of uniformity. Each of them, young and old, I
found, had his own distinctive persona within a corporate
existence, dedicated, equally, to study and meditation, manual
labour and worship. What good are they doing? What future
have they got? Prayers don't show in the Gross National Product,

and so cannot be said to lighten the Chancellor of the Exchequer's burdens. Nor do they, like napalm and hot air, serve the cause of freedom in any perceptible way. They cannot be projected like guided missiles, or sent like sputniks to explore the physical universe. Telly-deprived, denied access to the treasures of the daily and periodical press, how can the monks be expected to have meaningful views on the birth pill, LSD, the Stones and other burning issues of the day?

As for their future—the *Zeitgeist* is against them; in an increasingly materialist world they are non-productive citizens. Their prayers and anthems so ardently intoned are only for God, and he, as various eminent theologians have learnedly explained, is either dead or has tiptoed away from our world, leaving it to us. Yet somehow I remain unconvinced. By all the laws of Freud and the psycho-prophets, the monks are depriving themselves of the sensual satisfactions which alone make a whole life possible; they ought to be up the wall and screaming. Actually, I found in Nunraw a quite exceptional peace; it is the children of affluence, not deprived monks, who howl and fret in psychiatric wards.

The day ends for the monks with Compline at 7.30. As they leave their chapel after singing it, the Abbot shakes holy water over them. Then they retire to bed. I usually sat up for an extra hour or so, reading, thinking, or just looking out of my window. No heavenly visitation befell me, there was no Damascus Road grace; and yet, I know, life will never be quite the same after my three weeks with the Cistercians at Nunraw.

Observer, 20 August 1967

A LIFE OF CHRIST

I. THE BIRTH

It was somewhere here, in the neighbourhood of the present-day Bethlehem, that Christ's birth took place; on any showing, the most momentous event in the history of our Western civilisation.

In the exposition and portrayal of it, literally billions of words, oceans of paint, acres of canvas, mountains of stone and marble, have been expended, not to mention, in recent times, miles of film. Is there, then, anything left to say? I ask myself, rather disconsolately, and decide that there is—not because of me, but because of him. The man and his story are inexhaustible, and continue to attract the minds and the imaginations of the pious and the impious, of believers and unbelievers, alike; mine among them.

Christ's mother, Mary, conceived him out of wedlock, but believed when an inner voice, or angel, told her that her pregnancy was divinely ordained. Joseph, a poor carpenter from Nazareth who married her, likewise understood that the child to be born to her had a special destiny in the world. Every son of every mother is a son of God, but Mary knew that her son was to have a unique relationship with God and a unique role in the lives of men. She expressed her joy in this knowledge in the greatest of all the songs of motherhood; the more wonderful because, in her particular case, the circumstances of the birth-to-be were so dubious and so lowly:

My soul doth magnify the Lord, and my spirit hath rejoiced in God my Saviour.

For he hath regarded the lowliness of his handmaiden:

For, behold, from henceforth all generations shall call me blessed.

For he that is mighty hath magnified me, and holy is his name.

It was to this couple that Christ was born, coming into the world, as all of us do, to the accompaniment of cries of physical pain and inward spiritual ecstasy. As Blake put it:

My mother groaned, my father wept.
Into the dangerous world I leapt.

The place—a stable or outhouse, a cave, maybe—no other more suitable accommodation being available, or within the meagre means of Mary and Joseph.

Beneath the Church of the Nativity in Bethlehem, a silver star marks the alleged precise spot where Christ was born. A stone slab nearby is supposed to be the actual manger where he lay. The Holy Land is littered with such shrines, divided up, like African colonies in the old colonialist days, between the different sects and denominations—the Greeks, the Armenians, the Copts, the Latins, etc.—and often a cause of rancour between them. Most of the shrines are doubtless fraudulent, some in dubious taste, and none to my liking. Yet one may note, as the visitors come and go, ranging between the devout and the inanely curious, that almost every face somehow lights up a little. Christ's presence makes itself felt even in his alleged birthplace.

The essential point, as I see it, about Christ's birth is that it was so poor and so humble. The Son of God was born into the world, not as a prince, but as a pauper. So, to deck up the legendary scene of his nativity with precious hangings, pictures, glittering lamps and other ornamentation, is to destroy whatever valid symbolism it might otherwise have. Truly, we human beings have a wonderful faculty for thus snatching fantasy from the jaws of truth.

I find it marvellous that the Christian religion should thus have begun, from a worldly point of view, so inauspiciously in Bethlehem, where, despite her advanced pregnancy, Mary had come with Joseph from Nazareth because a census was being taken. Probably no child born into the world that day seemed to have poorer prospects than Christ did. It would have taken a perceptive eye indeed to see in the child in the manger one who was to be worshipped through the centuries by all conditions of men as their unique Saviour.

Some shepherds, we are told, watching their sheep in nearby fields—these fields, at least, unchanged and unadorned—were given the good tidings of great joy that Christ had been born, and rejoiced accordingly. There is also word of some wise men or kings from the East who came to Bethlehem bearing gifts of gold, frankincense and myrrh. Judging by our own wise men, I find difficulty in believing that any such would recognise God's son in Mary's. Let the vastly more numerous unwise go on marvelling at that stupendous moment in history when, for the first time, God was revealed to men, not in the guise of power or wealth or physical beauty, but of weakness, obscurity and humility.

Christ was born into a world as troubled as ours, and into one of its more troubled corners. The mighty Roman Empire, seemingly larger and more magnificent than ever, was already beginning to decompose, as even a carpenter's son on its periphery might vaguely realise. Then it was Jewish insurrectionists who made the trouble; today it is Jews ruling over their State of Israel who have to contend with Arab insurrectionists. According to the Gospel narrative, Joseph was induced to take Mary and her baby into Egypt to escape a murderous decree by King Herod ordering the killing of all children under two. If this indeed happened, they would not have been the first refugees in this part of the world—nor the last. One has a sense here of people endlessly on the move, carrying with them children and poor bundles of possessions—like the Arabs making their way across the River Jordan from the triumphant Israelis; displaced persons, to use our own sick expression, who haunt our twentieth-century feast of affluence. After Herod's death, Joseph settled in Nazareth, and it was here that Christ grew up. We know nothing of his childhood years and young manhood, and must assume that he received such formal education as he had from the rabbis. As they teach now, so, we may suppose, they taught then, basing themselves on the Law and the Prophets.

A few miles from Nazareth was the Lake of Galilee, teeming

with life and people. This was the countryside he knew, where the most important months of his life were to be spent. From the beginning he was aware of a special destiny to reveal to men the ways of God, and their duties one towards another, as all children of God. One cannot live by bread alone, he was to say, thinking, I dare say, of the bread and circuses, the avid pursuit of wealth and luxury, the permissive morality and eroticism, which characterised Roman society at that time, as it does ours today.

Each generation of Christians inevitably seeks to fashion its own Christ; from the austere figures carved in wood of the early Middle Ages, through the ebullient Renaissance Christs, to the weird efforts of our own time, sometimes clerically sponsored, to devise a Hipster Saviour. Yet behind all this there is a real man; born, growing up, reaching maturity like other men; turning his mind, as I have tried to turn mine, to what life means rather than to what it provides; trudging through this self-same dust, and sheltering from this self-same sun; lying down at night to sleep, and rising in the morning to live another day.

I, too, have my notion of what he was like—this man in whose flesh God deigned to live and die. I seem to catch a glimpse of him on these hill-tops, ever looking for new horizons; I note a vague suggestion of him in the face of some young rabbi. Did I hear his voice coming from afar, faintly across the Lake of Galilee? Is that his dust where some solitary traveller disappears into the distance? Here, where he lived, the very air I breathe carries his words—those sublime words about losing one's life in order to save it, about how it is the spirit that gives life while the flesh profits nothing; words which have changed human life and history as no other words ever have.

Christ's own circumstances were humble enough certainly—a carpenter's shop in Nazareth where he doubtless worked as a youth—but did not preclude awareness of the Roman Empire and all its luxury, self-indulgence and ostentation. Troops came and went; the Roman Governor lived in state at nearby Caesarea; King Herod had one of his pretentious palaces at

Tiberias by the Lake of Galilee; there were the games, and all
the riff-raff who followed them, and the pagan gods and their
rites. How the rabbis must have hated it all; alien then, as now,
to their strict monotheism! The Jews bore their yoke as subject
people as best they might, with the added humiliation that their
own ruler, Herod, shared all the Roman vices and lived ob-
sequiously in the shadow of Roman power. It was the messianic
hope, written into their scriptures, undying through the centuries, which kept alive in them the prospect of deliverance
from their Roman conquerors as they had been delivered from
past ones.

We must assume that Christ, as a Jew, resented the Romans'
presence in his country, and looked askance at the cities they
built there—like Caesarea, where the Roman Governor, Pontius
Pilate, lived in state. Their—to a Jew—idolatrous cults; their
luxury and vice, particularly the games (providing, like television today, vicarious thrills and excitement)—all this would
have been abhorrent to him.

Christ's mission on earth, however, reached far beyond considerations of national independence or servitude—to the roots
of power itself, and the fearful passion men have to dominate
other men. His famous answer to the trick question whether
the Jews should pay tribute to Caesar—that they should render
unto Caesar the things that were Caesar's and unto God
the things that were God's—removed him for ever from the
role of freedom-fighter in our modern sense. He was no Gari-
baldi or Tito or Gandhi. What he offered was a larger
freedom of the spirit, available even—perhaps especially—to
slaves. He proclaimed as the only true freedom *the glorious
liberty of the children of God*. He called men to a service that is,
itself, perfect freedom, releasing them from the gruelling en-
slavement to their own egos and appetites. All other freedoms,
once won, soon turn into a new servitude. Christ is the only
liberator whose liberation lasts for ever.

Since Christ's death a whole succession of Caesars have come
and gone, all demanding tribute. The ruins of their cities stand
one on top of another—great slag heaps of history, the past
piling up in dust. It is only now, centuries later, that Jews again

rule in Judea. They have become their own Caesar, and are busily constructing their own Caesareas.

In Christ's day the extreme Jewish nationalists, or Zealots, represented one reaction to Roman domination; another was to be seen in the exacting asceticism practised by sects like the Essenes, who sought illumination and escape from the world's humiliations and passions in the practice of drastic mortification of the flesh and total detachment. The chance discovery, in a cave near one of their monasteries in the neighbourhood of the Dead Sea, of scrolls belonging to the time of Christ clearly indicates a certain inter-relation between their teaching and his. As the pagan world moved to its close such ideas were prevalent; they always are when the vanity of earthly hopes and human glory is about to be luridly demonstrated once more in history's unfolding drama. Besides belonging to eternity Christ belonged to his times; on the outskirts of a dying civilisation he spoke of dying in order to live. Today, when our civilisation is likewise dying, his words have the same awe-inspiring relevance as they had then.

The most famous of the ascetics was John the Baptist, who in the style of the old Hebrew prophets denounced the backsliding of the Jews and the villainy of their rulers, sparing none, least of all Herod—a temerity which cost him his life. Many came to him in the desert where, we are told, he lived on locusts and wild honey; a burning and a shining light. Those who repented he baptised with the water of the River Jordan. Some of Christ's greatest sayings were to do with water; by the banks of the Jordan one can see why. There, water provides an irresistible image of life itself. What better way of expressing the everlasting quality of truth than to see it as living water which will quench thirst for ever—*Whosoever drinketh of the water that I shall give him shall never thirst; but the water that I shall give him shall be to him a well of water springing up into everlasting life.*

John the Baptist called for repentance, for, he proclaimed, *the kingdom of heaven is at hand.* He was, he said, quoting Isaiah, *the voice of one crying in the wilderness, Prepare ye the way of the Lord, make his paths straight.* When Christ came to

baptism, John recognised him at once as this Lord
ath he was to make straight. Then the wild anchorite,
raiment of camel's hair, drew back before the young
teacher from Nazareth and bowed his head. Christ, he said,
must baptise him; not the other way round. When Christ gently
insisted, he gave way, and with the utmost humility poured the
water of baptism over Christ's head.

At that moment a bird flew across the blue sky, indicating
God's joy in what had happened. Only in the natural may we
see the supernatural, and *vice versa*. A bird could not exist
without God, and through its existence proclaims God's. Not
even a sparrow, we are told, can fall to the ground without
causing God concern; all the material universe is, as it were, a
message in code from God, which mystics, artists and scientists
strive to crack, sometimes with a measure of success, but to
which Christ provides the key.

Christ was thirty years old when he received baptism at the
hands of John the Baptist; now he must dedicate himself wholly
to the mission for which he came into the world—preaching,
teaching and living out his destiny.

2. THE MINISTRY

With his baptism by John the Baptist in the River Jordan,
Christ became fully aware of what was expected of him. There
is a similar moment of illumination in the lives of artists when
they first fully realise all that can be done with sounds or
colours or words to convey life's innermost glory and anguish.
The task Christ knew he must undertake was the most stupendous of all—no less than to make known to men the ways of
God. In that sense, he *was* God come down to earth in the guise
of a man, or, alternatively, a man reaching up from earth to the
very mind and being of God. He was, at one and the same time,
God incarnate and man deified; in him time and eternity,
mortality and immortality, came together, and God's very
breath brushed against mortal flesh.

Christ withdrew alone to the desert to fast and pray in preparation for a dialogue with the Devil. Such a dialogue was inescapable; every virtue has to be cleared with the Devil, as every vice is torn with anguish out of God's heart. Christ found the Devil waiting for him in the desert, but what took place between them was really a soliloquy. When we talk with the Devil we are talking to ourselves.

First, the Devil suggested that Christ should use his heavenly powers to turn stones into bread. What an alluring prospect!— man's prime necessity effortlessly and plentifully provided. Christ, however, turned the proposal down on the ground that the body's hunger must be subsidiary to the spirit's.

Then the Devil proposed that Christ should resort to wonders —like going to the moon, or travelling faster than sound, or splitting the atom. Why not, he said, cast himself down from a high place, and God would see that the angels took care of him so that he landed safe and sound? No, Christ said, no; we must not tempt God.

Finally, the Devil showed Christ all the kingdoms of the world in a moment of time, and said: *All this power will I give thee, and the glory of them: for that is delivered unto me; and to whomsoever I will I give it.* All Christ had to do in return was to worship the donor instead of God—which, of course, he could not do. How interesting, though, that power should be at the Devil's disposal, and only attainable through an understanding with him! Many have thought otherwise, and sought power in the belief that by its exercise they could lead men to brotherhood and happiness and peace; invariably with disastrous consequences. Always in the end the bargain with the Devil has to be fulfilled—as any Stalin or Napoleon or Cromwell must testify. *I am the light of the world,* Christ said; power belongs to darkness.

After his decisive dialogue with Satan, Christ very humanly chose to begin his ministry in Nazareth, where he was known and had grown up. There in the synagogue, with I daresay his family present in the congregation, he chose to read the splendid passage in which the prophet Isaiah proclaims:

The Spirit of the Lord is upon me,
Because he hath anointed me to preach the gospel to the poor;

He hath sent me to heal the broken-hearted, to preach deliver-
     ance to the captives, and recovering of sight to the blind,
To set at liberty them that are bruised,
To preach the acceptable year of the Lord.

All would have been well if Christ had just left matters there. Nothing pleases the average congregation more—whether in synagogue, church, mosque or other conventicle—than to be told about preaching deliverance to captives, healing the broken-hearted, etc., always provided nothing is expected of *them*. But Christ went on recklessly : *This day is this scripture fulfilled in your ears*. In other words, *he* was going to do it; the spirit of the Lord was upon *him*, Joseph's son, known to them all. It was intolerable. With one accord they rose up and turned him out of the synagogue and out of Nazareth. As far as we know he never returned there.

He made for Capernaum by the Lake of Galilee. I see him, a solitary figure, trudging along, until the sight of the lake opened up before him; with no luggage, no money, no prospects, no plans; only those magnificent words still ringing in his ears, and a sense of exaltation at the knowledge that he had, indeed, been chosen to give them a new tremendous reality. Those who met him along the way must have marvelled to see one who was at once so poor and so uplifted.

In Capernaum he found his first disciples among the fishermen on the lake. They just dropped their nets and followed him. With, perhaps, a touch of dry humour (detectable from time to time in Christ's sayings, and to me very pleasing) he told them that thenceforth they might expect to catch, not fish, but men. What did they see in him?—someone of their own kind and class, yet inspired; saying to them things, simple and comprehensible in themselves, but such as they had never heard before—things which gave a new meaning and a new glory to their daily lives; a new dimension to life itself. *Never man spake like this man*. Who, then, could he be but the long awaited Messiah? They recognised him when others, cleverer and more important, were blind.

Some of the disciples, chosen then or later, were of a higher social and intellectual level than the fishermen—for instance,

Matthew, who sat *at the receipt of custom*; but the original twelve, the first Christians, must have presented a nondescript appearance. If Pilate, the Roman Governor, or Herod had happened to catch a glimpse of them, how could he possibly have guessed that they were, indeed, going to *turn the world upside down?*

Christ's life revolved round the Lake of Galilee during the succeeding months of his ministry. Each morning it was this scene which met his eyes; each evening he could watch the sun going down behind these self-same hills. Sometimes he preached from a boat on the lake, or escaped from too demanding crowds into the solitude it offered. Often he went by boat from one side to the other, for convenience, or for security reasons—to slip quickly out of the kingdom of King Herod, *that fox*, as he called him. I daresay he sometimes bathed in the lake. Certainly, he knew its storms and its calms; the hazards of a fisherman's life and the varying amounts of his catches.

Once he was seen, we are told, apparently walking on the lake's surface; on another occasion, he spoke into a furiously blowing wind, and it died down. It is not surprising that, after the Crucifixion, his spirit should have manifested itself to his disciples here by the lake where they had lived together. If there was one earthly scene which stayed with Christ, it was surely this one—Galilee.

Christ had a special concern for the sick and the infirm— *Come unto me all ye that labour and are heavy laden, and I will give you rest.* They gathered round him—the lame, the halt, the blind, the crazy—sometimes in embarrassing numbers, in the hope that his healing hands, or even glance, might fall on them and they would be cured. All the miseries of human life were his concern, and should, he said, be ours. If we turned aside from the unfortunate and the afflicted, we should be turning away from him—*Inasmuch as ye did it not to one of the least of these, ye did it not to me.*

What are we to make today of these miracles he performed which made so powerful an impact on his contemporaries— relieving the mad of the evil spirits which tormented them, restoring their sight to the blind, telling the bed-ridden that their sins were forgiven them so that there was nothing to stop them getting up and walking?

The world at all times is full of shattered or distorted bodies and minds (not least now, despite all that modern medicine can do). To them Christ offered, not medicine, but forgiveness; when he relieved them of their burden of guilt, he also automatically relieved them of their infirmities. We who believe in the magic of drugs, in the psychiatrists' mumbo-jumbo, find this hard to credit. Even the most violent of lunatics could be calmed by Christ's presence—like a poor fellow the Gospels tell us of who was so crazed and violent that he had to be bound with chains and fetters, and even then broke away and rushed naked into the desert. Christ ordered the evil spirits out of him, and they entered into a herd of Gadarene swine, who then ran violently down a steep place and were choked—providing an image for all time of the self-destruction of the human will.

I have always had the feeling that Christ did his miracles with a certain diffidence, sometimes even reluctance. That is to say, he was most human when, as in his miracles, he resorted to the supernatural, whereas it was in his life and his words that his divinity showed most clearly. Christ saw sickness as an aspect of the imperfection which belongs to the human situation. He came to show us perfection—a perfection to be realised, not by perfecting our bodily existence (supposing that to be possible), but by taking us out of our bodies and their exigencies altogether. As we slough them off, as a snake does an old skin, it matters little whether they are strong or weak, sick or well. Christ opened blind men's eyes, but he tells us that we are all blind, and shows us how to see. Even Lazarus, whom he raised from the dead, is but an image of the new life he offers to everyone who will die in the flesh and be reborn in the spirit. If cures were found for every disease ever known or to be known (a miracle far exceeding any achieved by Christ in his random essays as a healer), everything would be the same. We should still be blind and sick and crazy as long as we allowed ourselves to be preoccupied with the hopes and desires of this world.

Much of what Christ had to say in the course of his teaching and preaching was not new or original, but put with an exquisite grace which comes through the Gospel narratives, especially in our Authorised Version—on any showing, one of the greatest works of genius in the English language. People—especially the poor—flocked to hear him, recognising the authority with which he spoke, and uplifted by the prospect of living in a new way that he held out to them. No doubt, too, the apocalyptic aspect of his teaching appealed. We love to think the world is shortly going to end; it enhances our sense of importance to see ourselves as positively the last generation of men.

It was on a hill by the Lake of Galilee that the most famous of Christ's discourses was delivered—what has come to be called the Sermon on the Mount. Imagine the scene—in the evening hours, when the heat of the day is over, but the sun is still in the sky. Here they are gathered, eagerly climbing the hill; all buoyed up by the prospect of meeting him at the top—a bedraggled enough audience by comparison with the turn-out for the games in Tiberias below.

On one such occasion, we are told, Christ felt bound to provide food for them, miraculously turning some loaves and fishes a boy had with him into enough for the multitude. Or maybe—as I have sometimes imagined—it was just that, in the light of his words, those who had brought food with them felt constrained to share it with the others who hadn't. If so, it was an even more remarkable miracle. Thus to transform what we call human nature, releasing it from its ego-cage, is the greatest miracle of all.

So Christ began, and they listened with an enchantment the words still evoke after two thousand years:

Blessed are the poor in spirit: for theirs is the kingdom of heaven....

Blessed are the meek: for they shall inherit the earth....

Blessed are the pure in heart: for they shall see God.

Blessed are the peacemakers: for they shall be called the children of God.

And so on.

No words ever uttered, it is safe to say, have had anything like the impact of these, first spoken to some scores, maybe hundreds, of poor, and mostly illiterate people, by a teacher who, in the eyes of the world, was of small account; at best another John the Baptist, who, instead of taking to the desert and a diet of locusts and wild honey, lived humbly, but more or less normally, in Capernaum.

Christ turned the world's accepted standards upside down. It was the poor, not the rich, who were blessed; the weak, not the strong, who were to be esteemed; the pure in heart, not the sophisticated and the worldly, who understood what life was about. Righteousness, not power or money or sensual pleasure, should be man's pursuit. We should love our enemies, bless them that curse us, do good to them that hate us, and pray for them that despitefully use us, in order that we may be worthy members of a human family whose father is in heaven.

So Christ spoke. No one has fully carried out his sublime behests, but it is due to his words on a hill overlooking the Lake of Galilee all that long time ago, that some, at least, have tried. In the countryside where he lived and taught one is constantly reminded of the imagery he used—the sower going forth to sow, the lilies more glorious than Solomon in all his glory, the Good Shepherd leading his sheep and sometimes carrying one of them too weak or sick to walk, goats and sheep separated. Not even the exigencies of tourism, the multitudinous shrines, now under the aegis of the new twentieth-century State of Israel, have quite obliterated the scenes of daily life on which Christ drew by way of illustration to make his meaning clear.

What did they make of him, I wonder—his listeners by the Lake of Galilee. They were certainly curious, and certainly impressed. But did they understand? Did even the disciples understand? I doubt it. After all, we don't understand even now; if we did the world would be a quite different place, and the terrible things that have happened, and are happening, in our time would be inconceivable. What Christ had to say was too simple to be grasped, too truthful to be believed. Our faculties are like those smelting works which can only take ore of a high degree of impurity; when the light is too bright we cannot see.

So the great majority of Christians have never been able to believe that when Christ said the whole duty of man resolved itself into loving God and our neighbour, he meant just that. It seems too simple, too obvious. And, furthermore, there is the question of who is our neighbour. This was put to him slyly by a lawyer who hoped to trick him into differentiating between Jews and Gentiles. Instead, Christ told the parable of the Good Samaritan, using for its setting the road from Jerusalem to Jericho which, to this day, in its wildness, its remoteness and weird desolation, gives rise to thoughts of banditry such as befell the traveller who fell among thieves. This man's neighbour, Christ forces the lawyer to admit, was surely the Samaritan who helped him rather than the priest and the Levite who passed by on the other side. In Christ's estimation, our neighbour is everyone. *Feed my sheep*, he said— all, black, white and piebald. There are never any exceptions; if, as Christ taught, mankind is a family with one father in heaven, then it is inconceivable that anyone should be intrinsically of greater worth than another. As a Jew, Christ belonged to God's chosen people; as the son of God, he came to proclaim the universality of God's love.

During the years he spent on earth Christ was certainly recognised as a unique person—someone who spoke as no one else had ever spoken. Even in quite casual encounters—as with the woman of Samaria at the well—he made this impression, while his disciples who were constantly with him became convinced that he was the expected Messiah, the Son of God. Three of them—Peter, James and John—when they went to the top of a high mountain with him saw him visibly shining with the truth and inspiration that was in him, and seemed to hear him conversing with great figures from the past, with Moses and Elijah. Peter, ever impulsive, made the absurd suggestion that they should build three tabernacles on the spot, one for Christ, one for Moses and one for Elijah. On the contrary, Christ said, the incident should not even be mentioned, lest people should suppose that the enlightenment he brought might be magically attained, instead of seen with mortal eyes and grasped with mortal minds.

The time had now come for Christ and his disciples to go to Jerusalem for the Feast of the Passover, when, as he had known from the beginning, the last tragic phase of his human destiny would be fulfilled. There never was any question in Christ's mind but that he had to die; in his many silent sessions of prayer and communing with himself the mystery of the Atonement and his part in it had become clear to him. The world would have to destroy him in order that henceforth the nature of the world should be made manifest; he had to die, a victim to the blindness and cruelty and destructiveness of the human will, in order that succeeding generations of men should be shown a way of escape from such torment. His death was to be a birth; his end a beginning.

The road to Jerusalem was long and dusty; they took it together, this little band of obscure men, scarcely aware of the momentousness of their journey; how, out of it, would come a great new civilisation, refertilising the parched earth of paganism, reviving its withered hopes and spent dreams, until once more, centuries later, the same blight fell and the same rebirth was required. On through Jericho they went, past the Dead Sea, and up that benighted road Christ had used for his parable of the Good Samaritan, until at last, turning a corner, Jerusalem came into view, built on a hill, a welcome sight, a glorious destination:

> O Jerusalem, Jerusalem, thou that killest the prophets, and stonest them which are sent unto thee, how often would I have gathered thy children together, even as a hen gathereth her chickens under her wings . . .

Two of the disciples were sent ahead to get a donkey, and on it Christ rode into the city, thronging with Passover celebrants. Some of them recognised him, knowing of his fame in Galilee, and began to shout *Hosanna*! and to spread their garments and to tear down palm branches and strew them in his way. It was the nearest thing to a political demonstration that Christ ever encountered, and if there had been the tiniest grain of demagogue in him he would have responded accordingly. Had he so responded, it would have been the end of his mission. The world would have had to await another Saviour. I imagine him half smiling, knowing, as he did, that the same throats shouting *Hosanna!* would shortly be shouting *Crucify him!* with the same zest and the same fatuity.

3. THE ROAD TO EMMAUS

In Jerusalem Christ's mood was different—sterner and sadder; at times almost bitter. Every evangelist must believe in his heart that if only he tries hard enough to deliver his message people will pay heed. Surely, what seems so clear to him will be clear to others! The hungry sheep look up, and he longs to feed them. Then he realises that even when they do follow, it is usually for the wrong reasons. They will, as readily, follow any other shepherd who comes along, true or false. Christ did not know, when he lived on earth, but could easily have guessed, that before he had been long dead men would be killing other men in his name, and setting golden crowns on the heads of popes and kings to his greater glory.

What, I have occasionally asked myself, would the man whose fortunes we have been following have made of the Vatican or Lambeth Palace or the House of Lords? Christ was the Good Shepherd; he was listened to, certainly, but Tiberias, Capernaum, Caesarea, Jerusalem itself, went on their way regardless. In earthly terms, his mission was a failure; now he had to fulfil it in God's way—which led to the cross.

I see Christ on the Mount of Olives, looking across at Jerusalem, deeply stirred as any Jew must be, because of its tremendous place in Jewish life and history. The city was very different then, of course, with the huge magnificent temple dwarfing everything else, and the towers of Herod's palace rising into the sky. Different, and yet the same; then, as now, a place of violence, of furious passions and bigotries. Roman soldiers patrolled the uneasy streets as Israeli ones do today; strictly orthodox rabbis, or Pharisees, scornfully eyed their laxer fellow-Jews, stonily averting their gaze from the Gentiles in

82   JESUS REDISCOVERED

their midst, precisely as I've seen them doing on their way to
the Wailing Wall—all that remains of their once splendid
temple, where they ceremonially bemoan its passing, as well as
all the transitoriness and unsatisfactoriness of human life.
Strange, majestic, bearded men, to me rather appealing, who
resolutely refuse to accommodate themselves to the twentieth
century which their more pliable countrymen have brought to
their ancient city.

What could Christ do about Jerusalem—except die there? In
his eyes, the city was as surely moving towards destruction as
the Gardarene swine when he sent evil spirits into them—its
fine buildings, its crowded streets, its synagogues, the temple
itself, all doomed to destruction. So, like the Hebrew prophets
of old, Christ foresaw the wrath to come, which duly came—
army after army sweeping in, the latest a Jewish one; the temple
razed to the ground, to provide a site for other temples dedicated to other Gods than Jehovah—now a mosque; Jerusalem
destroyed, to rise again and be destroyed again.

It was as though here was the world's soul, where all its
bitterest conflicts and most searching dilemmas must be worked
out; whence would come also its truest understanding and
sweetest hopes. Looking over at Jerusalem from the Mount of
Olives and thinking of all this—of the suffering and privations
involved, of the narrow path God has set to salvation, Christ
wept.

It was in such a mood that Christ drove the money-changers
out of the temple. We all know the feeling—the blind rage that
human beings should sully every place and everything with
their hateful little cupidities. I confess that I have felt it in the
Holy Land at the relentless exploitation of shrines and relics
and credulities for gain. If I'd had the nerve I might well have
hurled a stock of crowns of thorns at the head of their vendor!
The next day, we may be sure, the money-changers were back
in their places plying their trade as zealously as ever. They are
at it still—in banks and stock-exchanges, in casinos and bingo-
halls, wherever the money-game is played—that's everywhere.

Christ liked to walk out from Jerusalem in the evening to
nearby Bethany rather than stay in the city, where he was

always in danger, and where—as I like to think—he felt choked and oppressed by the dust and restlessness of the streets. In Bethany there were two sisters, Mary and Martha, and their brother Lazarus whom, when he was thought to be dead, Christ had called forth from the tomb itself. One gets from the Gospels a delightful picture of this household where Christ was always welcome. The sisters were quite different in temperament—Mary thoughtful and imaginative, Martha practical and energetic. On one occasion, when Mary was seated at Christ's feet and listening to him with rapture, Martha, *cumbered about much serving,* humanly grew irritated. I see her in her working clothes, sleeves turned up, face flushed from the fire where she was preparing with loving care a supper she knew her guest particularly liked.

Lord, she expostulated, *dost thou not care that my sister hath left me to serve alone? Bid her therefore that she help me.*

Christ's answer was perfect: *Martha, Martha, thou art careful and troubled about many things; but one thing is needful; and Mary hath chosen that good part, which shall not be taken away from her.* It was Mary who subsequently poured a whole pound of very costly spikenard ointment over Christ's feet, and wiped them with her hair, earning a rebuke from, of course, Judas, who spoke on behalf of all charitable prigs at all times when he complained that the money spent on the ointment should have been given to the poor. In Christ's reply one may detect again that note of astringent irony I like so much—*Let her alone: against the day of my burying hath she kept this. For the poor always ye have with you; but me ye have not always.* It is all perfectly described, and bears upon it every mark of truth.

Christ and his disciples celebrated the Passover together in the traditional way. Now he knew that his hour was drawing near, and insisted on washing the others' feet, showing them once more that every act of true humility is a sort of grace whereby the soul grows as the will, or ego, diminishes. Whosoever would be great in this world, he was always telling them, is small; and whoever, through his sense of God's greatness, realises his own smallness, becomes spiritually great.

As things turned out, it was to be their last Passover; it was also—though, of course, they didn't know it—the first Communion service. For the first time those mysterious words were spoken:

> *Take, eat; this is my body. . . . this is my blood of the new testament, which is shed for many for the remission of sins. . . .*

Words to be endlessly repeated, in every language, to the accompaniment of every variety of ritual, or in stark simplicity. At this original austere Last Supper, Christ showed how, through the Blessed Sacrament—the bread he broke and the wine he sipped with his disciples—he would remain always within our reach.

Thus the Christian religion was born here in Jerusalem two thousand years ago. It has brought to the world, as Christ said it would, not peace but a sword. Jerusalem itself remains a place of strife and fratricidal conflict, and Christianity's ostensible devotees remain divided and flounder, tragically and often absurdly, in their rivalries and uncertainties. *In the world,* Christ said to his disciples, *ye shall have tribulation.* A generation like ours, which has seen the two most destructive and cruel wars of history, and all that followed from them, will not be inclined to question the inevitability of tribulation.

Christ, however, did not stop there. *But be of good cheer,* he went on, *I have overcome the world.* So he had, not as earthly conquerors do, by force of arms or fraudulent promises; rather, by seeing through the world, and the evanescence of its hopes and desires, and the utopian dreams which embody them. He showed us how to escape from the little dark cell our egos make, so that we may see and hear and understand, whereas before we had been blind and deaf and dumb.

It was at the Last Supper that Christ indicated his awareness that one of his disciples would betray him. He even pointed to Judas as being that disciple; Judas knew that Christ knew, and yet he could no more draw back than Macbeth could from murdering Duncan or Vronsky from seducing Anna. Mystics and great artists know—what is often hidden from other men—

that our free will is shaped by our passions into an inescapable destiny. Prometheus is both bound and free.

At the Last Supper, too, Christ told Peter that that very night, before the cock crew, he would deny him thrice. Never! said Peter indignantly; never, never, never! Alas, poor Peter! He was, of course, subsequently forgiven, to become, as many Christians have believed, the rock on which Christ's Church would be built, *and the gates of hell shall not prevail against it.*

Christ now went with three of his disciples to the Garden of Gethsemane, below the Mount of Olives. His soul, he said, was *exceeding sorrowful, even unto death,* and he wanted to be alone and to pray. So he left the disciples to sit and wait for him, and withdrew by himself. The earth's shapes and sounds and colours and living creatures, we should remember, were not less dear to Christ because of his divine destiny than they are to us; rather more so, if anything. To leave them behind, to die, so early in his earthly life, was still a deprivation even though his death was to put an end for ever to dying in the old pagan sense of finality.

We cry when we leave our homes to venture out into a world we long to explore. So Christ was sorrowful that the time had come when he must leave loving friends and disciples, the road to Bethany in the deepening dusk, the Lake of Galilee and the fishing boats coming in with their catches—all the familiar scenes and dear companionship he had known on earth. *O, my Father,* he prayed, *if it be possible, let this cup pass from me: nevertheless, not as I will, but as thou wilt,* reflecting, as he must have done, how easy it would be for him to slip away by himself, back to Galilee, and a happy private life there like other men, with a wife, children and all the other mitigations of the loneliness and mystery of our human fate. How easy, and how impossible!

He found the disciples asleep, and rebuked them rather irritably: *What, could ye not watch with me one hour?* Then he again went off by himself to continue with his prayers, returning to find them once more asleep. This time he let them be. What did it matter now? Soon the Garden of Gethsema resounded with the noise of a mob armed with swords and staves (a few days before it had been palm leaves) who were looking for him. Judas, to earn his thirty pieces of silver, proceeded to identify him with a kiss and a *Hail, Master!*—and Christ was apprehended. Someone drew a sword in his defence, but Christ quickly told whoever it was to put up his sword, *for all they that take the sword shall perish with the sword*. Thereupon, we are told, *all the disciples forsook him and fled*. He was alone.

Now began for Christ the farce of the judicial proceedings against him, intended to give his execution a show of legality. There is, of course, no such thing as earthly justice, and cannot ever be; only the will of the strong over the weak, dressed up with more or less propriety according to the antiquity of the procedure. Judges have to wear wigs and robes—as Pascal pointed out—to hide the inadequacy of the justice they dispense, which would otherwise be all too apparent. Christ maintained a contemptuous silence while witnesses of sorts were being cross-examined at the house of Caiaphas, the High Priest, where he had been taken. It was only when Caiaphas asked him point-blank if he was the Christ, the Son of God, that he deigned to reply, and then only to say: *Thou hast said*.

It was enough. *Blasphemy!* Caiaphas shouted. There was no need to hear any more witnesses, he went on, and asked those standing by what they thought. *He is guilty of death*, they obediently answered, and proceeded to mock and insult Christ, and knock him about, in a style that has become all too familiar in the various utopias of our time.

That same morning Judas tried to return his thirty pieces of silver to the priests and elders who had given him them, but they would not receive the money back. So he threw the coins on the temple floor and went and hanged himself; a man, it seemed, on whom all the darkness in the universe had settled. Was he, too, forgiven at last—a beneficiary from the death he helped to bring about? Surely Christ died even for Judas.

The High Priest and the elders were not entitled to impose the death sentence; so they took Christ, bound, to Pontius Pilate, who was.

What was the cause of their relentless hostility to Christ? Neither his messianic claims, nor his occasional Jewish unorthodoxies, it seems to me, account for the bitter resentment he aroused in them. There were others at that time in Judea who claimed to be Messiahs, and for the most part Christ conducted himself like a strict and pious Jew.

No, as I see it, Christ's real crime was simply that he spoke the truth, which is intolerable to all forms of authority—but especially ecclesiastical. *Ye shall know the truth, and the truth shall make you free,* Christ said. In the eyes of Caiaphas and his associates, as later in the eyes of Dostoevsky's Grand Inquisitor, Christ had to die because the truth he spoke and the freedom he offered undermined the authority other men claimed and exercised.

When Pilate—to me the embodiment of every colonial governor that ever was, so that I see him in a grey frock-coat and topper—asked Christ whether he was King of the Jews, he replied: *To this end was I born, and for this cause came I into the world, that I should bear witness unto the truth.* Pilate, no fool, was impressed. *What is truth?* he muttered, and went out to Caiaphas's men to tell them that he found no fault in Christ, and to suggest that he should be released on the occasion of the Passover. No! they shouted, No! Give us Barabbas!—a Jewish partisan who was also due to be crucified. Pilate shrugged and gave way; it didn't matter much to him either way. How surprised he would have been to know that this obscure affair would keep his memory alive centuries after the Roman Empire he served had ceased to exist.

Now the Roman soldiers, bored with the whole affair, indulged in a sick joke. They stripped Christ and put a scarlet robe on him; then crowned him with a crown of thorns, affecting to pay him homage: *Hail, King of the Jews!* As so often happens with sick jokes, theirs rebounded on their own heads. Had they but known it, in making fun of this King of the Jews, they were mocking, not Christ, but their own caesar, and every caesar, king or ruler that ever had been or was to be. They were making power itself derisory for ever. Thenceforth, for all who had eyes to see, thorns sprouted underneath every golden crown, and underneath every scarlet or purple robe there was stricken flesh.

There followed the Crucifixion. Christ humped his cross along the *Via Dolorosa* (if that was indeed the way he took to Golgotha) until he was too weak to continue, when another took it for him. Three crosses were set up, with Christ's in the middle and a thief on either side, and the long agony began. The crowd of spectators, I imagine, consisted, as such crowds usually do, of the curious, the morbid and some casual passers-by. In this particular case, there were doubtless a few of Caiaphas's men to keep the jeering going and some Roman soldiers. A group of women, we are told, stood on the outskirts —his mother, Mary Magdalene and others from Bethany and Galilee. At one point he was given vinegar to drink; just before he died he was heard to cry out in a loud voice: *My God, my God, why hast thou forsaken me?*

Thus ostensibly it all ended in defeat and despair. 'Well, that's all over,' Caiaphas and his friends must have thought. How wrong they were! It was only beginning. Not defeat, but a fabulous new hope, had been born; not despair, but an unexampled joy, had come into the world. Christ died on the cross as a man who had tried to show his fellow-men what life was about; he rose from the dead to be available for ever as an intermediary between man and God.

How, rose from the dead? After his death on the cross, we are told, he was seen by the disciples and others on numerous occasions; the stone in front of the tomb where he was laid was found to have been removed, and the tomb to be empty. These are matters of legitimate historical investigation; what is not open to question is that today, two thousand years later, Christ is alive. The words he spoke are living words, as relevant now as when they were first spoken.

Shortly after Christ's death on the cross, two men were walking along the road to Emmaus, a village some seven or eight miles distant from Jerusalem. One of them, Cleopas, may have been connected by marriage with Christ's family. As they walked along they naturally talked about the Crucifixion and its aftermath; so absorbed in their talk that they scarcely noticed when a third man drew alongside and walked with them. He broke in to ask them what they were talking about so earnestly, while looking so sad.

Obviously, Cleopas said, he must be a stranger if he hadn't heard of the recent happenings in Jerusalem. Then they told him how Christ had been crucified (although they, Cleopas and his companion, had *trusted that it had been he which should have redeemed Israel*), and how certain women of their company had gone to the tomb where he had been laid, and found it empty, seeing at the same time a vision of angels who said that he was alive.

Thereupon the stranger went through the scriptures with them, showing that everything that had happened had been foretold. By this time they had reached the house in Emmaus they were making for, and the stranger would have gone on alone, but the others pressed him to stay with them *for it is toward evening, and the day is far spent*. He accepted their invitation. When they sat down to seat, and he broke bread and blessed it, they recognised him at last. He was no stranger, but their Saviour. Then he disappeared. Cleopas and his companion could not even wait to finish their meal, but hurried back full of joy and hope to Jerusalem, along the road they had so lately travelled, to tell the others of their marvellous experience. On every walk, Christ came to tell us, whether to Emmaus or Wimbledon or Timbuktu, there is the same stranger waiting to accompany us along our way, if we want him.

The rest of the story of Christ belongs to history. Terrible things have been done in his name; the doctrine of unworldliness which he preached has been twisted to serve worldly purposes; the cross on which he died, besides inspiring some of the noblest lives which have ever been lived, and some of the noblest thoughts and creations of man, has also served as a cloak for some of the basest; his gospel of love has been enforced with the rack and the whip, and driven home with the sword.

Let others better qualified than I work out, if they can, the gain and the loss, in human terms. Here, where he was born, lived and died, we may remember how miraculously, none the less, his light continues to shine in the dark jungle of the human will, as I—a true child of these troubled times, with a sceptical mind and a sensual disposition, most diffidently, unworthily, but with the utmost certainty—testify.

The Commentary of three television programmes.
B.B.C. 2; 10, 11 and 12 April 1968

FOUR SERMONS

I. ANOTHER KING . . .

Nowadays when I occasionally find myself in a pulpit—one of those bad habits one gets into in late middle-age; and never, by the way, in a more famous pulpit than this one—I always have the same feeling as I look round as I do now at your faces; a deep, passionate longing to be able to say something memorable, to shed some light.

I am the light of the world the founder of the Christian religion said. What a stupendous phrase! And how particularly marvellous today when one is conscious of so much darkness in the world! *Let your light shine before men,* he exhorted us. You know, sometimes on foolish television or radio panels, or being interviewed, someone asks me what I most want, what I should most like to do in the little that remains of my life, and I always nowadays truthfully answer, and it *is* truthful, 'I should like my light to shine, even if only very fitfully, like a match struck in a dark cavernous night and then flickering out.'

How I should love to be able to speak to you with even a thousandth part of the certainty and the luminosity of St Paul for instance in Thessalonica, when he and his companions were, in the most literal sense, turning the world upside down by insisting, contrary to Caesar's decrees, that there was another king, one Jesus. Golden words, a bright and shining light indeed. Now something had happened to him, as it had to Christ's disciples, transforming them from rather inarticulate cowardly men who ran away for cover when their leader was arrested, into the most lion-hearted, eloquent, quick-witted, yes, and even gay evangelists the world has ever known. Irresistible in their oratory, indomitable in their defiance, captivating in their charm; overwhelming in the love which shone in their faces, in their words and in their deeds. Well, what had happened to them? We can call it what we like as far as I'm concerned—'the Holy Ghost descending,' 'Damascus Road conversion,' 'speaking with tongues,' anything you like, I don't mind. The point is that, as they said themselves, they were reborn. They were new men with a new allegiance, not to any form of earthly authority but to this other king, this Jesus. Ever since their time, with all the ups and downs, confusions and villainies of institutional Christianity, this notion has persisted, of being reborn, of dying in order to live, and I want to consider whether such a notion, as I understand it the very heart of the Christian religion, has any point or validity today.

In the boredom and despair of an expiring Roman civilisation, with all the inevitable accompaniments of permissive morality, addiction to vicarious violence, erotic and narcotic fantasies, it offered a new light of hope, a new joy in living, to one and all, including, perhaps especially including, the slaves. In our uncannily similar circumstances, has it anything to offer today? That's my question. Of course I can't answer it as St Paul and the disciples did. They were the beginning; we are the end. I, too, belong to the twentieth century, with a twentieth-century sceptical mind and sensual disposition, with the strange mixture of crazy credulity in certain directions, as for instance in science and advertising (if you happen to cast an eye through the advertisements in your colour supplements you will see displayed there a credulity which would be the envy of every witch-doctor in Africa) and equally crazy scepticism, so that illiterate schoolboys and half-baked university students turn aside with contemptuous disbelief before propositions which the greatest minds and the noblest dispositions of our civilisation—Pascal, say, and Tolstoy—accepted as self-evident. That is our twentieth-century plight. Let me then, in true twentieth-century style, begin with a negative proposition—what I consider to be the ineluctable unviability and absurdity of our present way of life.

How can anyone, apart from an occasional 'with it' cleric, provost of King's or Hungarian economist, seriously believe that by projecting present trends into the future we arrive at enduring human felicity—producing more and more and consuming more and more year by year under the impetus of an ever more frenzied persuasion by mass-communication media, and at the same time watching the rest of mankind get hungrier and hungrier, in ever greater want; growing ever stronger, with the means at our disposal to blow ourselves and our earth itself to smithereens many times over, and at the same time becoming ever more neurotic about the imminence of global nuclear war; moving ever faster and farther afield, exploring the universe itself, and pursuing happiness, American style; 'grinding out our appetites,' as Shakespeare so elegantly put it, ever more desperately, with physical and even moral impunity, and spiritual desolation. It is a state of affairs at once so bizarre and so tragic that I alternate between laughing hilariously at it and looking forward eagerly to my departure from the scene, quite soon now—in at most a decade or so. This year, at sixty-five years old, I move into the N.T.B.R. (Not To Be Resuscitated) bracket, when some high-minded, highly skilled doctor will look me over and decide in his infinite wisdom and humanity whether I am worth keeping alive. As I have said, I alternate between a sense of the utter absurdity of it all and a desire to get out of so nonsensical a world.

May I, moving from general things to more particular ones, consider for instance the situation in this ancient university, with which through the accident of election I find myself briefly associated. The students here in this university, as in other universities, are the ultimate beneficiaries under our welfare system. They are supposed to be the spearhead of progress, flattered and paid for by their admiring seniors, an élite who will happily and audaciously carry the torch of progress into the glorious future opening before them. Now, speaking for myself, there is practically nothing that they could do in a mood of rebelliousness or refusal to accept the ways and values of our run-down, spiritually impoverished way of life, for which I shouldn't feel some degree of sympathy or, at any rate, understanding. Yet how infinitely sad; how, in a macabre sort of way, funny, that the form their insubordination takes should be a demand for Pot and Pills; for the most tenth-rate sort of escapism and self-indulgence ever known! It is of one of those situations a social historian with a sense of humour will find very much to his taste. All is prepared for a marvellous release of youthful creativity; we await the great works of art, the high-spirited venturing into new fields of perception and under-standing—and what do we get? The resort of any old slobber-ing debauchee anywhere in the world at any time—Dope and Bed.

The feeling aroused in me by this, I have to confess, is not so much disapproval as contempt, and this, as you may imagine, makes it difficult, in fact impossible, for me as Rector to fulfil my functions. Here, if I may, I should like to insert a brief word of personal explanation. I, as Rector, and Allan Frazer as my Assessor, find ourselves as you know responsible for passing on to the university authorities the views and requests of the student body as conveyed to us by their elected officers, and as set forth in their magazine *Student* for whose conduct they are responsible. Their request concerning the handing out of birth pills is as it happens highly distasteful to us, as we have not hesitated to let it be known. The view of the S.R.C. officers as expressed by some of them, and not repudiated publicly by any of them, is that the Rector and his Assessor are bound not only to pass on but to recommend whatever the S.R.C. may decide. This is a role which, in my opinion, no self-respecting Rector, or Assessor, could possibly countenance, and I have therefore asked the Principal to accept my resignation, as has my Assessor.

So, dear Edinburgh students, this is likely to be the last time I address you, and this is what I want to say—and I don't really care whether it means anything to you or not, whether you think there is anything in it or not. I want you to believe that this row I have had with your elected officers has nothing to do with any puritanical attitudes on my part. I have no belief in abstinence for abstinence's own sake, no wish under any cir-cumstances to check any fulfilment of your life and being. But I have to say to you this : that whatever life is or is not about, it is not to be expressed in terms of drug stupefaction and casual sexual relations. However else we may venture into the unknown it is not I assure you on the plastic wings of *Playboy* magazine or psychedelic fancies.

I have recently, as you might have heard, been concerned in making some films for B.B.C. television on the New Testament, and it involved, along with much else, standing on what purports to be, and, unlike most shrines, may well be, the Hill of Beatitudes where the most momentous of all sermons was preached some two thousand years ago. It was rather marvellous standing there looking down on the Sea of Galilee and trying to reconstruct the scene—the obscure teacher and the small, nondescript, mostly illiterate crowd gathered round him. For the Christian religion began, let us never forget, not among brilliant, academic minds, not among the wealthy, or the powerful, or the brilliant, or the exciting, or the beautiful, or the fascinating; not among television personalities or leader-writers on the *Guardian*; it began among these very simple, illiterate people, and one was tremendously conscious of them gathered there.

And then those words, those incomparable words, which were to echo and re-echo through the world for centuries to come; even now not quite lost! How it is the meek, not the arrogant, who inherit the earth. How we should love our enemies, and do good to them that hate us. How it is the poor, not the rich, who are blessed, and so on. Words which have gone on haunting us all even though we ignore them; the most sublime words ever spoken.

One of the Beatitudes that had for some reason never before impressed me particularly this time stuck in my mind and has stayed there ever since. It is: *Blessed are the pure in heart for they shall see God.* May I commend this Beatitude to you as having some bearing on our present controversies and discontents. To see God is the highest aspiration of man, and has preoccupied the rarest human spirits at all times. Seeing God means understanding, seeing into the mystery of things. It is, or should be, the essential quest of universities like this one, and of their students and their staff. Note that the realisation of this quest is achieved, not through great and good deeds, nor even through thought, however perceptive and enlightened, certainly not through sensations, however generated, nor what is called success, however glittering. The words are clear enough— *Blessed are the pure in heart for they shall see God*.

To add to the macabre comedy of our situation, into the ribald scene of confusion and human inadequacy that I have been talking about there break idiot voices prophesying a New Jerusalem just round the corner. One always, I find, under-estimates the staying power of human folly. When poor old H. G. Wells breathed his last, having produced in *Mind at the End of its Tether* a final repudiation of everything he had ever said or thought, I fondly supposed, and said to myself, that no more would be heard in my time of men like gods. How wrong I was! A quarter of a century later a provost of King's, Cambridge, was to carry the same notion to an even higher pitch of fantasy. No doubt, long after I am gone someone will be saying on some indestructible programme like 'Any Questions?' that a touch more abortion, another year at school, and birth pills given away with the free morning milk, and all will be well.

What are we to do about it, this crazy Gadarene slide? I never met a man made happy by money or worldly success or sensual indulgence, still less by the stupefaction of drugs or alcohol. Yet we all, in one way or another, pursue these ends, as the advertiser well knows. He offers them in Technicolor and stereosound, and there are many takers. The politician likewise, often with a nondescript retinue of academic and clerical support, offers the same package in collective terms. Underneath, we all know how increasingly hollow and unconvincing it is— the Great Society, mankind coming of age, men like gods, all the unspeakable cant of utopians on the run. Our very art and literature, such as they are, convey the same thing—the bad dreams of a materialistic society. Bacon and Pinter tapering off into the sheer incoherence of a Burroughs and a Becket, with the Beatles dancing on our grave, and Allen Ginsberg playing his hand harmonium, and that delectable old Hindu con-man, the Maharishi, throwing in his blessing. Communist utopianism produced Stalin; the pursuit of happiness, American style, produced Richard Nixon, and our special welfare variety has produced Harold Wilson. If that doesn't put paid to all three nothing ever will. As for the scientific utopia looming ahead, we have caught a glimpse of that, too, in the broiler houses, the factory farms and lately the transplant operations, with still warm bodies providing the spare parts for patching up others, and so *ad infinitum*.

So I come back to where I began, to that other king, one Jesus; to the Christian notion that man's efforts to make himself personally and collectively happy in earthly terms are doomed to failure. He must indeed, as Christ said, be born again, be a new man, or he's nothing. So at least I have concluded, having failed to find in past experience, present dilemmas and future expectations, any alternative proposition. As far as I am concerned, it is Christ or nothing.

To add a final touch of comic relief (because you know an ex-editor of *Punch* cannot help, even in the most gruesome situations, looking around for something comic), I might add that what I have just said is, I know, far more repellent to most of the present ecclesiastical establishment than any profession of scepticism or disbelief.

I increasingly see us in our human condition as manacled and in a dark cell. The chains are our mortal hopes and desires; the dark cell is our ego, in whose obscurity and tiny dimensions we are confined. Christ tells us how to escape, striking off the chains of desire, and putting a window in the dark cell through which we may joyously survey the wide vistas of eternity and the bright radiance of God's universal love. No view of life, as I am well aware, could be more diametrically opposed to the prevailing one today, especially as purveyed in our mass-communication media, dedicated as they are to the counter-proposition, that we *can* live by bread alone, and the more the better. Yet I am more convinced than I am in my own existence that the view of life Christ came into the world to preach, and died to sanctify, remains as true and as valid as ever, and that all who care to, young and old, healthy and infirm, wise and foolish, with or without 'A' or 'O' levels, may live thereby, finding in our troubled, confused world, as in all other circumstances and at all other times, an enlightenment and a serenity

D

not otherwise attainable. Even though, as may very well prove the case, our civilisation like others before it soon finally flickers out, and institutional Christianity with it, the light Christ shed shines as brightly as ever for those who seek an escape from darkness. The truths he spoke will answer their dilemmas and assuage their fears, bringing hope to the hopeless, zest to the despairing and love to the loveless, precisely as happened two thousand years ago and through all the intervening centuries.

I finished off my filming in the Holy Land by taking with a friend the road to Emmaus. Those of you who still read the Bible will remember the details—how, shortly after the Crucifixion, Cleopas, some sort of relative of Christ's family, and a friend were walking from Jerusalem to Emmaus and inevitably talking as they went along about the Crucifixion which had happened so recently. They were joined by a third man who fell into step beside them and shared in their conversation. When they arrived at their destination in Emmaus, since it was late they pressed him to come and eat supper with them. The story, you know, is so incredibly vivid that I swear to you that no one who has ever tried to write can doubt its authenticity. There is something in the very language and manner of it which breathes truth. Anyway, they went in to eat their supper, and of course when the stranger broke bread they realised he was no stranger but their Saviour. As my friend and I walked along like Cleopas and his friend, we recalled as they did the events of the Crucifixion and its aftermath in the light of our utterly different and yet similar world. Nor was it a fancy that we too were joined by a third presence. And I tell you that wherever the walk, and whoever the wayfarers, there is always this third presence ready to emerge from the shadows and fall in step along the dusty, stony way.

*Delivered at the University of Edinburgh Service
in the High Kirk of St Giles, 14 January 1968*

2. LIVING WATER

It is a curious fact that today, as I have found, one is called a pessimist if one ventures to express a certain contempt for the things of this world, and dares to entertain the truly extra-ordinary hopes about our human destiny which buoyed up the first Christians when, in earthly terms, their master had gone from them and their cause was lost. What a weird reversal, as I should have thought, of common sense! What a preposterous distortion of language! How, I ask myself, can it be pessimistic to call in question the transitory satisfactions available in our mortal existence, and to contrast them with the enduring ones offered us in the Gospels and Epistles? I wonder whether, in the history of all the civilisations that have ever been, a more insanely optimistic notion has ever been entertained than that you and I, mortal, puny creatures, may yet aspire, with God's grace and Christ's help, to be reborn into what St Paul calls *the glorious liberty of the children of God*. Or if there was ever a more abysmally pessimistic one than that we, who reach out with our minds and our aspirations to the stars and beyond, should be able so to arrange our lives, so to eat and drink and fornicate and learn and frolic, that our brief span in this world fulfils all our hopes and desires.

Is it to be supposed that the woman of Samaria after her encounter with Christ—so exquisitely recounted by St John—didn't remember, every time she drew water at Jacob's Well, about that other living water she had been told of; that water which, once drunk, left one never thirsting again—a well inside one, and springing up everlastingly? In the same way, how can one who has glimpsed, however fleetingly, what King Lear calls 'the mystery of things', that *life of the soul* to which Isaiah refers—how can such a one ever again be wholly serious about mere worldly pursuits like fame and sensual pleasure and money, even though the colour supplements, all the different manifestations of this dreadful Frankenstein of mass-communication media that we have constructed, aim ceaselessly to persuade us that these pursuits alone make life worth while! I may,

I suppose, regard myself, or pass for being, a relatively success-ful man. People occasionally stare at me in the streets—that's fame. I can fairly easily earn enough to qualify for admission to the higher slopes of the Inland Revenue—that's success. Furnished with money and a little fame even the elderly, if they care to, may partake of trendy diversions—that's pleasure. It might happen once in a while that something I said or wrote was sufficiently heeded for me to persuade myself that it re-presented a serious impact on our time—that's fulfilment. Yet I say to you, and I beg you to believe me, multiply these tiny triumphs by a million, add them all together, and they are noth-ing—less than nothing, a positive impediment—measured against one draught of that living water Christ offers to the spiritually thirsty, irrespective of who or what they are. What, I ask myself, does life hold, what is there in the works of time, in the past, now and to come, which could possibly be put in the balance against the refreshment of drinking that water?

I ventured to cite my own case. Let me cite another infinitely more impressive. I can never forget reading, when I was a young man, in Tolstoy's Confessions of how, working in his study, he had to hide away a rope that was there, for fear he should use it to hang himself. To me at that time it seemed extraordinary. Here was the greatest writer of modern times; someone of whom, as a young aspiring writer myself, I thought with the utmost veneration; whose work seemed (and seems) to me so marvellous that if in the course of my life I managed to write something even a hundredth part as good as the shortest and most desultory of his short stories, I should be well content. And here was this man, of whom Gorky said that as long as Tolstoy lived he could never feel an orphan in the world; here was this man of incomparable gifts and greatness—rich, courted, with a large family, a loving wife, every worldly blessing that anyone could possibly aspire to—unable to endure the sight of a rope because it reminded him of how he might end a life which had grown insufferable. Why insufferable? Because he was assailed by the hopes and desires of the world—even more desolating, as he well knew, in realisation than in aspiration. Because he seemed to be alone and afraid in an alien universe. Then, as he recounts, he lost himself in Christ's love, from which, St Paul tells us, nothing can separate us if we hold fast—not tribulation, not distress, not persecution, not famine, not nakedness, neither peril nor sword. Tolstoy, as we know, did hold fast, becoming not only the greatest writer, but also one of the greatest Christians, of modern times. He earned thereby, inevitably, the relentless hostility of his country's Church and its hierarchy, but he had the incomparable satisfaction of devoting his sublime genius, not just to diverting his contemporaries, enriching himself and feeding his own vanity, but to keeping alive the sweet truths Christ died to teach us—of forgiveness, of brotherliness, of love of God and of our fellows, dying to this world and being reborn as new men with new values, new hopes and a new inexpressible joy in the destiny Christ came on earth to reveal to us. He could repeat with a steady voice St Augustine's prayer—so infinitely touching to anyone who, however unworthily and inadequately, has tried to communicate in the spoken or the written word : *Let me offer you in sacrifice the service of my thoughts and my tongue, but first give me what I may offer you.*

We must look, it seems to me, for comedy in all things; the builders of our mediaeval cathedrals knew what they were doing when they stuck grinning gargoyles on their majestic edifices, and, as Chesterton pointed out, the Fall of Man is only the banana-skin joke carried to cosmic proportions. Now here's a funny thing! If I'd been talking in this sort of strain in this Scottish pulpit a century ago, there would have been nothing surprising or out-of-the-way in the sentiments I expressed, though some eyebrows might, admittedly, have been raised, at such excessive praise of a Russian writer who, whatever other merits he might have, was emphatically not a Scottish Presbyterian. Today it is otherwise. Many of the leaders and clergy of the various Christian denominations are insistent that Christ's kingdom, contrary to what he said, *is* of this world, and that treasure laid up on earth to be distributed ever more lavishly to the citizens of an affluent consumer society is of the greatest possible moment. Anyone who suggests that the pursuit of happiness—that disastrous phrase written almost by chance into the American Declaration of Independence, and usually signifying in practice the pursuit of pleasure as expressed in the contemporary cult of eroticism—runs directly contrary to the Christian way of life as conveyed in the New Testament, is sure to be condemned as a life-hater, one who blasphemously denigrates God's world and the creature—man—made in his image.

Unspeakable clergymen twanging electric guitars denounce him; episcopal voices cast him into outer darkness; from without, and sometimes within, the churches comes insistence that to be carnally minded is life; that it is the flesh that quickeneth and the spirit that profiteth nothing. I speak here, I may add, about what in some small degree I have experienced myself. It was from the Roman Catholic chaplain of Edinburgh University and a number of his associates that there came the bitterest denunciation of myself as Rector and of my Assessor and friend, Allan Frazer, for having resigned rather than seem to countenance a demand for the indiscriminate distribution of contraceptives to the students. To the best of my knowledge no Church dignitary (with the honourable exception of the Free Church of Scotland) spoke up in public on our behalf, though one or two wrote to us privately in sympathetic terms. There are many other and much more important instances of the same sort. These induce me to say in all honesty that, in my opinion, the Church leaders and clergy have made such concession to prevailing permissive *mores* and materialism that, unless there is a quick and dramatic reversal of their present attitudes, I personally shall be very surprised if a decade or so from now anything remains of institutional Christianity—an outcome which quite a number of them openly hope for. Here, at least, their hopes are likely to be realised.

If, indeed, the Christian religion rested upon the word of these leaders, and the ostensible Christian consensus they are struggling to achieve, I should long ago have abandoned all faith in its survival. In fact, of course, Christianity's validity lies in its own inherent and everlasting truth. What the living Christ signified and signifies to men will endure even though the Vatican is another ruin with the Coliseum, and tourists are poking about the debris of Lambeth Palace as now they do about Herod's. No doubt a racy foreword by the Emperor Tiberius would have helped to popularise St Paul's Epistles, and if the apostles had adjusted their teaching to current depravity they might have reached a larger audience. Their practice was the precise opposite; asking everything on Christ's behalf—a total surrender of the ego, a putting aside of the preoccupations of this world, a death to be followed by a rebirth—they were according everything. On the other hand, experience shows that those who ask little tend to be accorded nothing—a saying which may well be the epitaph of twentieth-century institutional Christianity.

When one comes to the social application of this new-found sanguine attitude to man's earthly circumstances one enters upon a scene of pure fantasy, so outrageously ribald as to defy satire itself. If the directors of the vegetarian movement were to petition the Worshipful Company of Butchers for affiliation, it would not be nearly as funny as the spectacle of the Church's involvement in the notion of material progress, political liberation and the realisation through the exercise of power and the creation of wealth of a kingdom of heaven on earth. How I envy the historian who, like Gibbon, will look back across the centuries at the hilarious spectacle of Marxist-Christian dialogues attempting to find common ground between the brutal atheism of the Communist Manifesto and the Sermon on the Mount; of pious clergymen attaching themselves to enraged mobs shouting for Black Power or Student Power or some other crazed shibboleth; of an Anglican bishop in gaiters recommending *Lady Chatterly's Lover*. Such lunacy, I assure you, is the despair of professional comedians.

The trouble with earthly causes is that they, alas, are liable sooner or later to triumph. Turn your minds for a moment to the unhappy plight of those so-called Christian Socialists who identified the rise of the Labour Party with the coming of Christ's kingdom. What must be their feelings today? Or those others who saw in Soviet Communism the fulfilment of Christian hopes—what must they feel as the full villainy of Stalin's regime becomes manifest? All purely human hopes are fraudulent, as their realisation in purely human terms must always prove deceptive. As the Magnificat so splendidly puts it, the mighty are put down from their seats and the humble and meek exalted; but never forget that these same humble and meek, once exalted, become mighty in their turn and fit to be put down.

Fantasies like these belong to the half-light before night falls. I have no wish to luxuriate in apocalyptic prognostications, yet it would seem obvious enough that the last precarious foothold of law and order in our world is now being dislodged. We may expect the darkness. Such were precisely the circumstances in which the Christian religion was born; they may well provide for its rebirth. In the Holy Land today one is confronted on every hand with the debris of the great Roman Empire and world order which in Christ's time seemed so strong, widespread and dominant. Who could have foreseen in those days that the words of an obscure teacher in a remote outpost of the empire would provide the basis for a new and most glorious civilisation—the two thousand years of Christendom now drawing to a close; that his squalid death by execution would inspire the noblest thoughts, the most sublime art, the most disinterested dedication and exquisite love the world has yet known. Likewise, today who can tell what comes after us—who have made ourselves so strong and feel so weak and helpless, who have become so materially rich and spiritually impoverished, who know so much and understand so little! I think of a man, Paulinus, in the fourth century about whom I have read. Foreseeing the darkness ahead he decided to light a lamp and keep it burning in a Christian shrine. I should dearly love to do just this—a little lamp to signify that whatever the darkness, however profound the sense of lostness, the light of Christ's love and the clarity of his enlightenment still shines, and will continue to shine, for those that have eyes to see, a heart to love and a soul to believe.

Delivered in Queen's Cross Church, Aberdeen,
26 May 1968

3. UNTO CAESAR

I see that I've been billed to speak to you about Christianity and world problems. Let me explain straight away that I don't believe there are such things as world problems, but only a problem of man and his existence in this world. Furthermore, that if there were world problems, I am extremely sceptical as to whether there is, or can be, a specifically Christian answer to them. The relevant incident in the New Testament here is, of course, the putting of the question to Christ whether it was lawful to pay tribute to Caesar. His reply—highly ingenious and, I should suppose, partly ironical—to the effect that we should render to Caesar the things that are Caesar's and to God the things that are God's, neatly evaded the point at issue — Jewish nationalism. There is, I know, a school of thought, by no means without clerical support, which sees Christ as a sort of Che Guevara, and I fully expect yet another translation of the New Testament to be produced soon in which it is made clear that previous ones have erred in not indicating that Christ was a militant Jewish nationalist. The caesars to whom Christ said tribute was due have long ago disappeared, and today, two thousand years later, Jewish nationalism is at last triumphant in Jerusalem. Neither circumstance, as far as I'm concerned, has the slightest bearing on the message Christ came to deliver, the life he came to live and the death he came to die.

What, then, is our brief existence here on earth about? The media—I mean television, the colour supplements, the magazines, the newspapers; all the different organs of this immense apparatus of persuasion which has been developed in our time—answer the question with the utmost clarity and gusto. It's about being successful in terms of money, sex and fame, with violence thrown in for kicks. As trendy, sexy, affluent children of our time we may consider ourselves as living to the full. By the same token, if we are out of the swing, physically unattractive and poor, we must consider ourselves as outcasts and deprived. Anyone who has lived at all in the real world must have understood that this fantasy of the media is a total absurdity. This is not a happy age, even—perhaps particularly—for its greatest ostensible beneficiaries. The parts of the world where the means of happiness in material and sensual terms, are most plentiful—like California and Scandinavia—are also the places where despair, mental sickness and other twentieth-century ills are most in evidence. Sex, fanned by public erotica, under-pinned by the birth pill and legalised abortion, is a primrose path leading to satiety and disgust; the rich are usually either wretched or mad, the successful plod relentlessly on to prove to the world and to themselves that their success is worth having; violence, collective and individual, bids fair to destroy us all and what remains of our civilisation.

These judgments are not, I assure you, theoretical ones. I have worked in the media for the last forty years; I know how they function, the men who operate them and the motives which govern them. I have even held in my hands some of their prizes. If I say to you that these prizes are worthless, that far from enriching life they impoverish it, I am speaking from direct, personal experience. You will, of course, not believe me; as Pascal points out, it is part of the irony of our human situation that we ardently pursue ends which we know to be worthless. Why, even at my age, and utterly convinced of the truth of what I have just said to you, I can still aspire after applause and public recognition, when it has been demonstrated to me again and again in the most emphatic and unmistakable manner that such satisfactions only create a deeper, more agonising hunger than the one they are meant to allay. Even the great Augustine, with years of sanctity behind him, with one of the finest minds of his own or any other time, so passionately enrolled in the service of his God and his Saviour—even he could still be dragged with a silken thread into the blind alleyways of the senses. I think of him looking out of his window at Hippo on the Mediterranean, marvelling at its grandeur, at—as he puts it—the changing colours it slips on and off like robes, and reflecting that if such beauty as this is for us unhappy, punished men, what will the rewards of the blessed be like? It is so vivid, so human, so splendid.

Is there an escape route? Many are recommended today. For

instance, what is called Protest, an escape through mere destructiveness and lawlessness—Down with everything and everyone, including us! Then again, escape on the plastic wings of narcotics and erotica. Or escape through inertia—just refusing to join in; lying inert in the bottom of the boat with the bilgewater, indifferent as to where it's going and who holds the tiller. I feel a certain sympathy with, or at any rate understanding of, all of these escape routes, but I have to say to you that they're all cul-de-sacs. They lead nowhere. When the lawlessness and destruction have been achieved, the choice is between chaos and tyranny, and, faced with such a choice, the great majority of human beings will always choose tyranny, or have it imposed upon them. The plastic wings soon break, and those who relied on them to be lifted into the sky fall a dead weight on to the ground; the drop-out in the end becomes a bore to himself and to everyone else.

A more seemingly promising escape route is through the notion of social or collective regeneration. We are to agitate for a juster, more equitable, more brotherly society in which the wicked things like war, racialism, economic exploitation, all forms of unnecessary human suffering, are eliminated. This is where the world problems come in. We march through the streets chanting in unison 'Ho, Ho, Ho Chi-minh!', thereby, as we fondly suppose, helping to promote his victory in the Vietnam war and the defeat of American imperialism. We barrack Mr Enoch Powell when he tries to explain what he is getting at, thereby striking a blow against apartheid and segregationists everywhere. And so on. This sort of virtue has the great advantage, from the point of view of many clerics and secular evangelists, that it is a soft sell. How difficult, how desperately difficult, to curb one's so insistent ego, to put aside pride and vanity and follow the way of the cross! How easy, how really almost fatuously easy, to support Ho Chi-minh and be against Mr Powell!

Perhaps because it is so easy, the pursuit of collective virtue, ardently pursued over the last half century, has been singularly disappointing in its results. Two world wars, numerous revolutions, much political endeavour directed towards humanising our economic and social arrangements, have not resulted in a kinder way of life for Western man; still less for mankind as a whole. Who that is honest surveying the happenings of recent decades—the millions and millions who have been killed or uprooted from their homes, the wanton destruction, the almost inconceivable cruelties of a Hitler and a Stalin, the crazed quest for wealth and excitement—can seriously maintain that we are moving forwards spiritually, morally or even materially? This has been the century of the Kingdom of Heaven on Earth; many and varied have been its prophets and its guises—the American Way of Life, the Welfare State, the New Civilisation which people like Shaw and the Webbs detected in the monstrosities of Stalin—but what has come to pass, I fear, is better described as the Kingdom of Hell on Earth, soon, I should suppose, to pass into oblivion, its piled-up radioactive dust one more monument to the folly of man when he supposes that his destiny is in his own hands.

Utopianism, I am glad to note, is decidedly on the wane—though some dons and half-baked students continue to traffic in it. Thus, few any longer suggest, as the flower of our intelligentzia did up to quite a short time ago, that paradise has been regained in the U.S.S.R. Immigrants to the United States go there nowadays in search of a more affluent, not a better, life; our own Welfare State finds its only heralds—such as they are—among sociologists and statisticians. Even the protesting young feel constrained to fix their hopes on Mao Tse-tung because he is a long way away and little is known about him, rather than on more vulnerable saviours nearer at hand. The trouble with all earthly causes, however admirable they may be in intent, however earnestly promoted by their advocates, is that they are liable to triumph. Hugh Kingsmill, a writer whom I greatly admire puts it like this:

What is divine in Man is elusive and impalpable, and he is easily tempted to embody it in a collective form—a church, a country, a social system, a leader—so that he may realise it with less effort and serve it with more profit. Yet the attempt to externalise the kingdom of heaven in a temporal shape must end in disaster. It cannot be created by charters or constitutions, nor established by arms. Those who set out for it alone will reach it together and those who seek it in company will perish by themselves.

Turning aside, then, from delusive prizes and utopias which have been found wanting, what are we left with? Only our Christian faith. Let me conclude by trying to tell you, as briefly and simply as I can, what this means to me. I speak as someone unlearned in theology and philosophy. The various dogmas of institutional Christianity—like, for instance, the doctrine of the Trinity, or of the Immaculate Conception—just do not impinge; I neither believe nor disbelieve them, and feel no inclination to defend or denounce them. I find them perfectly comprehensible, perfectly harmless, and—as far as I'm concerned—totally without significance. Nor does the historicity of the Gospels' account of Christ's birth, life and death worry me at all. If, tomorrow, someone were to unearth another Dead Sea Scroll proving that, in earthly terms, the traditional Christian story just didn't happen in that way at that time, it wouldn't disturb my attitude to Christianity at all. Legends, in any case, seem to me more relevant to our human situation, and in that sense more 'factual', than history, which is really only the propaganda of the victor. Thus—by way of example—I find the Book of Genesis, considered as legend, infinitely more prescient on the subject of the origins and subsequent unfolding of our human story than, say, the theory of evolution, considered as fact.

I see Christianity as a very bright light; particularly bright now because the surrounding darkness is so deep and dense; a brightness that holds my gaze inexorably, so that even if I want to—and I do sometimes want to—I can't detach it. Christ said he was the light of the world, and told us to let our light shine before men. To partake of this light, to keep it in one's eye as the Evangelist told Bunyan's Pilgrim to do, is Heaven; to be cut off from it is Hell—two experiences as recallable and describable as was getting up this morning and driving to Oxford. Away from the light, one is imprisoned in the tiny, desolate dungeon of one's ego; when the light breaks in, suddenly one is liberated, reborn. The shining vistas of eternity open before one, with all mankind for brothers and sisters—a single family with a father in heaven, all, in the truest sense, equal, and deserving of one another's abiding love and consideration.

Words, just words! I can hear you saying. Well, yes, words; but there's something else—a man, who was born and lived like us; whose presence and teaching have continued to shine for generation after generation, just as they did for his disciples and for all who knew and listened to him in Galilee all those centuries ago. A man who died, but who none the less, in some quite unique way, remained, and remains, alive. A man who offered us the mysterious prospect of dying in order to live; who turned all the world's values upside down, telling us that it was the weak, not the strong, who mattered, the simple, not the learned, who understood, the poor, not the rich, who were blessed. A man whose cross, on which he died in agony, became the symbol of the wildest, sweetest hopes ever to be entertained, and the inspiration of the noblest and most joyous lives ever to be lived.

And now? Well, all I can say is, as one ageing and singularly unimportant fellow-man, that I have conscientiously looked far and wide, inside and outside my own head and heart, and I have found nothing other than this man and his words which offers any answer to the dilemmas of this tragic, troubled time. If his light has gone out, then, as far as I am concerned, there is no light.

Delivered in the Chapel of Hertford College, Oxford,
3 November 1968

4. MEN LIKE GODS

I want to speak to you today about what I regard as the one vital question of our time. This, put very simply, is: Is God in charge of our affairs, or are we? A great, and growing, body of opinion, some of it ecclesiastical, much of it in worldly terms powerful and influential, takes the view that *we* are now in charge. Whereas formerly it was considered man's highest aim to understand God's purpose for him, and his highest achieve-

ment to fulfil that purpose, now we are urged to dispense with
God altogether, and assume control ourselves of the world, the
universe and our own collective and individual destiny. God, we
are told—if he ever existed—has died; as a concept, he is not
needed any more. We know enough now about our environment and circumstances, have sufficient control over them, to
take over. Our apprenticeship is served; mankind has come of
age, and the time has come for us to assume command of ourselves and our world in our own right.

Let me say at once that I regard this notion as nonsensical,
and, if persisted in, as likely to have disastrous consequences.
The image of man puffed up to imagine himself a god occurs
frequently in legend and literature and history. Even in the
Garden of Eden the serpent tells Eve that if she eats of the
Forbidden Tree she and Adam *shall be as gods*. The Roman
emperors in their folly insisted on being worshipped as deities;
and in our own time a whole succession of squalid dictators
have arisen claiming an authority beyond reason, and even
beyond sense. Far from becoming gods, Eve's disobedience led
to her and Adam's expulsion from the Garden of Eden—she in
sorrow to bring forth children, he to till the ground from
whence he was taken. The deified Roman emperors are remembered, if at all, not as deities but as figures of absurdity and
fantasy in the pages of Gibbon, and we have watched our
contemporary dictators go one after the other to their unspeakable and ignominious ends. Was it not Icarus who thought to
fly into the sky on his wings of wax and feathers, only to have
them melted as he approached the sun, so that he fell like a
plummet into the sea? Not even Christ would allow the disciples to call him good, *because there is none good but one, that
is, God,* and at Lystra when the priests of Jupiter wanted to
offer sacrifices to Paul and Barnabas, they rent their clothes and
said: *Sirs, why do ye these things? We also are men of like
passions with you, and preach unto you that ye should turn
from these vanities unto the living God*.

None of these instances is likely to deflate the pretensions of
a twentieth-century scientific mind, with its extraordinary blend
of knowledge, dogmatic arrogance and infantile credulity,

though one may note with a certain pleasure that even so ardent
an upholder of men like gods as Dr Edmund Leach has lately
been voicing a certain anxiety about the human take-over. 'Unless,' he writes, 'we teach those of the next generation that they
can afford to be atheists only if they assume the moral responsibilities of God, the prospects for the human race are decidedly
bleak.' Bleak indeed!

Science has seemingly achieved so much. We can travel with
the speed of light, we shall soon be visiting the moon and
exploring the Milky Way. We can send our words, and
even our smiles, flying through the air to be picked up ten
thousand miles away; we can turn back rivers, plant out deserts,
and abundantly and effortlessly satisfy every human require-
ment, from potato crisps to skyscrapers, from royal jelly to giant
computers. All this has happened in one lifetime. Is it surprising, then, that those who have brought it about should see
themselves, not as mere mortal men, but as very gods? That
they should take on the functions of a god, claiming the right to
decide whose life is worth protracting, and whose should be cut
short, who is to be allowed to reproduce, and who should be
sterilised; reaching with their drugs and psychiatric techniques
into the mind, the psyche, and shaping it to suit their purposes;
re-sorting the genes, replacing worn out, derelict organs with
new ones freshly taken from living flesh, fancying, perhaps, that
in the end even mortality will be abolished—as an old vintage
car can be kept on the road indefinitely by constantly putting in
new sparking plugs, dynamos, carburettors, as the old ones
wear out; even re-defining the moment of death to suit their
convenience so that we are to be considered dead when Dr
Christian Barnard says we are?

Is it not wonderful? And, of course, that is only a beginning.
Writers like Aldous Huxley and George Orwell have imagined
the sort of scientific utopia which is coming to pass, but already
their nightmare fancies are hopelessly out of date. A vast, air-
conditioned, neon-lighted, glass-and-chromium broiler-house
begins to take shape, in which geneticists select the best stocks
to fertilise, and watch over the developing embryo to ensure
that all possibilities of error and distortion are eliminated.

Where is the need for God in such a set-up? Or even for a
moral law? When man is thus able to shape and control his
environment and being, then surely he may be relied on to
create his own earthly paradise and live happily ever after
in it.

But can he? It's precisely here that the doubt arises. Let us
take a quick, cool look at the world these men like gods have
so far succeeded in bringing to pass. It's a world of violence
and destruction unparalleled in human history. Who can esti-
mate the lives that have been lost and uprooted in the ferocious
conflicts of our time; the buildings, the treasures of art and
learning which have been wantonly destroyed; the misery and
privations, the degradation of standards of truth and humanity
which have accompanied their upheavels. And what about our
present situation? Is it worthy of men like gods—with one part
of the world glutted and surfeited with an excess of everything
they need, or can be persuaded to need, and the rest of the
world getting hungrier and hungrier, more and more deprived
of their basic necessities? With vast resources of wealth and
research devoted to making ever more potent engines of destruction, while in Asia and Africa and Latin America what we
call in our Orwellian Newspeak the under-developed peoples of
the world lack the very minimal medical requirements and
personnel? I could go on and on. I tell you in all seriousness
that in my opinion posterity will find the utmost difficult in
believing that people belonging to a technologically developed
civilisation like ours could possibly have tolerated such a
situation in the world; still less that their affairs were in the
hands of men like gods. Men like apes, they'll prefer to
believe, and even that will seem rather hard on the apes.

Let's imagine some future historian looking back across
thousands of years at us and our fantasies, follies and credulities. What will he make of it all, I wonder, seeing us imprisoned in a fantasy of our own making; in a dream, like Caliban's, full
of sounds and sweet airs, so that when we wake (if we ever do)
we cry to sleep again? A dream presented in innumerable ways
and guises—in the written and the spoken word, in sound and
vision and colour; above all, of course, on television; that

E

mysterious image of ourselves, that gigantic exercise in narcissism, piped into our homes; first two-dimensional in black and white, then (as one of the American networks put it) in 'living colour'—whatever that may mean. The grass, I should explain, is not green enough for television, nor, for that matter, is the blood red enough. They both need reinforcement. Greener than green, redder than red—a dream indeed. I noted down some words of Machiavelli which seemed to me very much to the point : 'For the great majority of mankind are satisfied with appearances, as though they were realities, and are often more influenced by things that seem than by those that are.' The same notion is expressed by Blake in one of those couplets of his so packed with meaning, so luminous, that you can go on contemplating them to the end of your life without ever exhausting their significance :

> They ever must believe a lie
> Who see with, not through, the eye.

He might have had television in mind; the camera is the most potent instrument for seeing *with* the eye that's ever been devised, and just think of the lies—the lies upon lies upon lies— that it's been able to induce belief in !

Looked back at across the centuries, it will all seem even more hilariously comical than it does today, though I imagine our historian being somewhat at a loss to understand what lay behind our plunge into sheer fantasy which his researches revealed. They can't really have believed, he'll say to himself, that this notion of Progress they bandied about meant anything. That happiness lay along the motorways, and well-being in a rising Gross National Product. That birth pills, easy divorce and abortion made for happy families, and sex and barbiturates for quiet nights. There must, he'll conclude, be some other explanation; a civilisation must have been possessed by a death-wish which so assiduously and ingeniously sought its own extinction—physically, by devoting so much of its wealth, knowledge and skills to creating the means to blow itself and all mankind to smithereens; economically, by developing a consumer economy whereby more and more wants have to be artificially created and stimulated in order to take up an endlessly expanding production; morally, by abolishing the moral order altogether and pursuing the will-o'-the-wisp of happiness through satiety; spiritually, by abolishing God himself and setting up man as the arbiter of his own destiny. A big laugh there for our historian, I should guess, as, looking back, he notes how our generation of men proved the least like gods, the least capable of coping with the complexities and dilemmas of their time, of any that had ever existed on earth.

Am I then concerned to say that there is no possibility of deliverance from this world of fantasy that we have created? Is the endlessly repeated message of the media—that money and sex are the only pursuits in life, violence its only excitement, and success its only fulfilment—irresistible? Are the only available escape-routes all cul-de-sacs? There is a remarkable passage in Pasternak's *Dr Zhivago* in which the hero reflects that in a Communist society freedom only exists in concentration camps—in other words, that the only way to be free is to be imprisoned. The same notion is to be found at the very heart of the Christian religion—that the only way to live is to die. There *is* a way of deliverance, after all, but it lies in the exactly opposite direction to the one so dazzlingly sign-posted by the media —out of the ego, not into it, heads lifted up from the trough instead of buried in it, the arc lights pale and ineffectual in the bright light of everlasting truth.

This is the Way Bunyan's Pilgrim took from the Wicket Gate to Mount Sion, the Way that opened up for St Paul after the Damascus Road. It is, of course, open to everyone at all times and in all circumstances. I think of St Augustine watching from his diocese at Hippo in North Africa, first the fall of Rome (and, incidentally, there were plenty of enlightened people then to contend that Alaric was a fine fellow, and that hope lay in a dialogue with him), and then the barbarians moving towards Hippo itself. It looked like an end, but really, as we know, it was a beginning.

The Way begins where for Christ himself its mortal part ended—at the cross. There alone, with all our earthly defences down and our earthly pretensions relinquished, we can confront the true circumstances of our being; there alone grasp the triviality of these seemingly so majestic achievements of ours, like going to the moon, unravelling our genes, fitting one another with each other's hearts, livers and kidneys. There, contemplating God in the likeness of man, we may understand how foolish and inept is man when he sees himself in the likeness of God.

Delivered at St Aldate's Church, Oxford,
1 December, 1968

A VISIT TO LOURDES

Some years ago I went to Lourdes with Mike Tuchner and a
camera crew to make a film for B.B.C. television about the place
and the pilgrims. I confess I had no expectation that the experience, though interesting, would be other than melancholy.
Generally speaking, I dislike shrines—especially being told
about them—and distrust miracles.

Actually, from the moment I got on the train at Victoria (we
travelled to Lourdes with a party of pilgrims so as to be able to
film *en route*), I had an extraordinary feeling of light-hearted-
ness. I don't think I have ever in my life been in so cheerful a
company as this collection of the sick and the crippled, many of
them soon to die, and those who were looking after them. Even
the restaurant car waiters when we got to France—men, in my
experience, not notable for cheerfulness of disposition, especially
when serving breakfast in the early morning to passengers who
have just crossed the Channel—responded to the atmosphere.
Their smiles and prompt kindly service cannot have been due to
expectation of tips; from this point of view it is difficult to
imagine a less promising party than ours.

These people—the fortitude with which they endured their
afflictions, the joy with which life none the less filled them,
their compassion for those more stricken than themselves, above
all their serene confrontation of the prospect of death in the
certain knowledge of God's love and mercy—occupied my mind
and spirit much more than Lourdes as a place.

Places, as it happens, have never interested me much, as such,
and Holy Places, whether Bethlehem or Lourdes, tend to be
marred for me by the sellers of tawdry relics, the bric-à-brac of
piety, who gather around them. However, in the grotto where
St Bernadette is supposed to have had her vision—the very heart
of Lourdes—I found a marvellous stillness; not due, let me

hasten to say, to absence of people. Never a moment, day or night, when there are not some suppliants coming and going, or kneeling in prayer—as we found when we tried to film the grotto empty. For most of the time, in all seasons, it is teeming with people. No, the stillness is within, not without; wonderfully peaceful and uplifting. Human beings are only bearable when the last defences of their egos are down; when they stand, helpless and humbled, before the awful circumstances of their being. It is only thus that the point of the cross becomes clear, and the point of the cross is the point of life.

Were there any miracles? Any number—almost as many as there were pilgrims. The miracle of faith and the miracle of hope endlessly repeated; of faith that in the totality of our earthly lives we are all—the infirm and the whole, the sick and the well, the crazy and the sane—children of God participating equally in his loving care; of hope that, as such, our woes and afflictions are no more than bumps and scratches, scarcely to be noticed, soon to be forgotten.

There was even a tiny miracle for me. A woman asked me to go and see her sister who was very sick. So of course I went along. The sister was obviously at the point of death, and like any other glib child of twentieth-century enlightenment, I had nothing to say, until I noticed in the most extraordinarily vivid way, as in some girl with whom I had suddenly fallen in love, that her eyes were quite fabulously luminous and beautiful. 'What marvellous eyes!' As I said this, the three of us—the dying woman, her sister and I—were somehow caught up into a kind of ecstasy. I can't describe it in any other way. It was as though I saw God's love shining down on us visibly, in an actual radiance. That was my miracle at Lourdes, and whenever I hear the Ave Maria they sing there all the time—otherwise, I expect, a rather banal tune—I remember my miracle with great joy.

B.B.C. broadcast, 7 September 1965

LIGHTS IN OUR DARKNESS

I. PASCAL

Pascal was born six years after Shakespeare died. Yet it is possible, as I have found, to 'discover' him today as though he were a contemporary whose work, by chance, had not before come to one's notice. To me he has been a source of delight and enlightenment. His sublime intelligence, so wide in its range, so firm in its grasp of our human condition, at once so subtle and so simple, seems to me to combine the cool appraisal of a scientist with the imaginative understanding of a poet and the humility of a saint.

My own study of Pascal, such as it is, has been confined simply to reading him; particularly, of course, the *Pensées*, but also, less carefully, the *Lettres Provinciales,* and other occasional letters and compositions—for instance, the fascinating *Entretien avec M. de Saci.* I have for the French text the excellent Pléiade edition edited by Jacques Chevalier, and for an English translation Martin Turnell's likewise excellent edition of the *Pensées* (Harvill Press).

M. Chevalier and Mr Turnell, I am sure for the best possible reasons, use quite different arrangements of the *Pensées.* It would be nice for ignoramuses like myself, to have an edition with the equivalent English and French texts on facing pages. Pascal's French is so luminous (the nearest I know is Rousseau's), his sentences shine so brightly, that one scarcely needs to know the language to read them. All the same, facing texts would be helpful.

Now this desultory reading has been reinforced by two capable studies of Pascal and his work, by the late Abbé Steinmann, and by Dr Broome of Keele University. Both I have found extremely helpful. Abbé Steinmann's is, from a biographical point of view, fuller and more informative. I accept the judgment of Mr Turnell (who translated it from the original French) that it is the best of its kind available to the general reader. As originally published, it seems, it was a good deal longer, and the text has been subjected to cuts and some editing. My suspicious Protestant mind makes me wonder whether efforts may have been made to prune out some of the more controversial aspects, especially in connection with the Jansenist controversy, which got the Abbé into trouble with his ecclesiastical superiors when he was alive. Dr Broome, from my point of view, is more workmanlike and sensible, though he does not attempt to deal other than factually with episodes like Pascal's first conversion, which Abbé Steinmann handles with great skill and understanding.

Before reading Abbé Steinmann and Dr Broome, I had only read, in the way of biographical studies, the enchanting memoir of Pascal by his sister Gilberte Périer, and the briefer recollections of him by her daughter, Marguerite Périer. Also the interesting, but somewhat suspect, account of Pascal's death by Père Beurrier, the local priest who administered the last rites.

Dr Broome, I am sure, is right when he points out that Gilberte's memoir is more hagiography than biography. Even so, I have to say that, for me, there emerged from her pious, elegant sentences a living man, by no means faultless, but uniquely gifted with understanding, with a dauntless ardour for truth and a quenchless love for his fellows, both those who were near—sisters, friends, relatives—and all men, especially the poor and the maimed in body or in mind. I find it particularly touching when Gilberte expresses regret that her brother, because of ill-health, should have left his great design, his apologia for the Christian faith, undone, with only some scattered notes to show what it might have been. Dear Gilberte, she need not have worried. Four centuries later we can still make do with the notes!

Jacqueline, Pascal's other sister, had a sterner and more resolute disposition. Against her family's wishes, she became a nun at Port-Royal, the centre of Jansenism, and there came to play an important part in her brother's spiritual development. Yet her grace, charm and beauty (though she caught smallpox and her face was pitted) likewise reach one across the centuries. All the trio seem caught in some special light which abolishes time; one's sense of their presence is so actual that one feels one must have met them yesterday over a meal or out on a walk. Jacqueline died ten months before her brother, probably also of tuberculosis. He, at the time of his death, was in his fortieth year.

In that short lifetime Pascal invented the computer (*la machine arithmétique*), started the first public passenger service in Paris, mastered the problem of the vacuum, expounded his scientific and mathematical studies with such brilliance that it was considered by no means inappropriate to compare him with Aristotle, engaged in vituperative and extremely effective theological polemics with the Jesuits, and finally, in spite of appalling ill-health and pain, attained a serene relationship with God and with his fellows, in the process producing one of the great masterpieces of all time—the *Pensées,* a work of Christian apologetics before which the most sceptical mind, indulgent flesh and arrogant spirit stand defenceless.

Not bad in thirty-nine years and two months! Unlike Lord Snow, Pascal reached the conclusion that what is now our great sacred cow—science—was a cul-de-sac. The mathematics he had fallen in love with as a child (to the point that, forbidden Euclid as too self-indulgent, he invented the early propositions for himself) proved a broken instrument. His proud, defiant mind had to be humbled before it could know anything at all:

It is vain, O men, that you seek within yourselves the cure for your miseries. All your insight only leads you to the knowledge that it is not in yourselves that you will discover the true and the good. The philosophers promised them to you, and have not been able to keep their promise.... Your principal maladies are pride, which cuts you off from God; sensuality, which binds you to the earth; and they have done nothing but foster at least one of these maladies. If they have given you God for your object, it has only been to pander to your pride; they have made you think that you were like him and resembled him by your nature. And those who have grasped the vanity of such a pretension have cast you down into the other abyss by making you believe that your nature was like that of the beasts of the field, and have led you to seek your good in lust, which is the lot of animals.

Paul Valéry considered such sentiments intimations of a sick mind. If so, let me be sick! 'Those who believe' Pascal also wrote, 'that man's good lies in the flesh, and evil in the things that induce him to turn his back on the pleasures of the senses, deserve to become glutted with them and to die of them'—a proposition which, if he had lived a little longer, Valéry would have seen well on the way to being fulfilled.

Observer, 6 February 1966

2. KIERKEGAARD

'The human race has in the course of generations become ever more insignificant'—it is the kind of sentence I love; startling, apparently nonsensical, in direct opposition to all contemporary dogmas such as progress, evolution, etc., etc., yet to a discerning mind glowing with an inner truth of its own.

Kierkegaard's writings, and especially the *Journals*, abound in such sentences. Let me give some more examples:

'A passionate, tumultuous age will overthrow everything, pull everything down; but a revolutionary age that is at the same time reflective and passionless leaves everything standing but cunningly empties it of significance.'

'When truth conquers with the help of 10,000 yelling men —even supposing that that which is victorious is truth; with the form and manner of the victory a far greater untruth is victorious.'

'Everyone in whom the animal disposition is preponderant believes firmly that millions are more than one; whereas spirit is just the opposite, that one is more than millions, and that every man can be the one.'

'Christianity is discord with the world, but in the Christian is the peace of Christ.'

'The more superior one person is to another whom he loves, the more he will feel tempted (humanly speaking) to draw the other up to himself, but (divinely speaking) the more he will feel moved to come down to him. This is the dialectic of love.'

'It is so heartbreaking that Christ, who is the teacher of love, is betrayed—with a kiss.'

'When secular sensibleness has permeated the whole world as it has now begun to do, then the only remaining conception of what it is to be Christian will be the portrayal of Christ, the disciples and others as comic figures. They will be counterparts of Don Quixote . . .'

'The Holy Scriptures are the highway signs: Christ is the way.'

What was there in this weird, unhappy, cantankerous little Dane which enabled him a century and more ago, in the very springtime of 'science' ('that increasing mass of drivel,' as he called it), before the juke-boxes had started playing or the mushroom cloud been written across the sky, to see just what was happening and where we were going? How did he, a sort of de Tocqueville of the spirit, come to grasp so clearly that preoccupation with numbers (to vote, produce, consume, march, howl, stare and otherwise react to mass persuasion) would prove inimical to our civilisation and its religion, and that the Christian Churches themselves, particularly the Protestant ones, would eagerly promote their own extinction by perverting a spiritual, transcendental faith into a carnal, worldly one? By what alchemy was he able even then to detect in the lineaments of enlightenment and righteousness the wrath to come? To hear the death-watch beetle at work when clergy 'trapped in all the twaddle of temporality' preached a Christianity 'lived in harmony with the flesh?'

And what about this, a decade before Northcliffe was born and two decades before Beaverbrook?

I say it is especially the daily newspapers which labour at degrading men to be mere copies. As in a paper factory the

rags are worked together into a mass, so the newspapers tend
to smooth out every individual difference in men, all spirit
(for spirit is differentiation in itself, and consequently also
from others), in order to make them happy *qua numerus*, by
means of the life which is peculiar to the number—in everything like the rest. Here the animal creature finds peace and
rest, in the herd.

Kierkegaard was the seventh child of elderly parents, his
mother being his father's second wife, formerly a servant in his
house, and several months gone in pregnancy on their wedding
day. He was undersized, vulnerable, highly intelligent, comba-
tive, often malign and always somehow forlorn, as the children
of the elderly often are—Max Beerbohm, for instance. Kierkegaard's relations with his father were passionate and troubled,
and it has often been suggested that they were reflected in his
attitude to the Deity. It might be so, but it is just as possible
that Kierkegaard, like many another seeing soul, felt himself all
along an orphan here on earth, and so looked for a father elsewhere.

In any case, he became increasingly an oddity, with one
trouser-leg shorter than the other, given to high spirits and
sharp talk in public and to melancholia in private. After some
early disorderly behaviour he turned to the study of theology,
but never became a minister. Perhaps his obsessive loathing of
Bishop Mynster ('that liar of blessed memory') among other
things, stood in the way. He fell in love with Regine Olsen, and
despite his grotesque physique succeeded in winning her heart.
Thereupon he felt bound to renounce her, and thenceforth
dedicated his prolific literary output to her.

Another curious episode arose out of his friendship with
Meir Goldschmidt, editor of *Corsair*, a satirical and sometimes
scurrilous weekly, a Copenhagen *Private Eye* as it were.
Kierkegaard occasionally helped Goldschmidt with a piece of
information, and in consequence enjoyed immunity in the pages
of his magazine. Then one day he asked Goldschmidt to spare
him no longer, and for a whole year *Corsair* went for him
regularly, making cruel fun of all his peculiarities, including his
misshapen body. The campaign was so successful that the chil-

dren in the streets cried out after him, and his first name, Soren, came to be eschewed. Parents would admonish their children : 'Don't be a Soren !'

It is easy to say that he was looking for martyrdom, that he was sick. Yet how much less sick, properly speaking, than some golden-hued Scandinavian of today chasing his happiness out of an upper-storey window, or into an Ingmar Bergman film! 'Only when a man has become so unhappy, or has grasped the misery of this existence so profoundly that he can truly say, "For me life is worthless," ' Kierkegaard wrote, 'only then can life have worth in the highest degree.' As he continually points out, all that is most mediocre and contemptible in human beings derives from the pursuit of earthly happiness. It is the glory of Christianity to have denounced and defied this pursuit; the Christian who none the less goes crawling on his stomach to make his peace with happiness earns Kierkegaard's particular contempt.

Such is his message, assiduously and skilfully proclaimed during his short life (he died when he was forty-two) and echoing on ever more loudly after his death when events themselves so dramatically underline and expound it. Even in his lifetime he was heeded more than might be supposed; Ibsen's Brand is said to be based on him. To a bruised twentieth-century mind like Camus's he brings the balm of reconciliation with the true, terrible and sublime circumstances of human life; he liberates us from liberation, wrests despair from the idiot jaws of hope, and turns us away from the frantic noise of history and all its hopes and desires in search of other, fairer and more enduring vistas.

Observer, 1 January 1967

3. SIMONE WEIL

Lovers of Simone Weil's mind and writings are greatly beholden to Sir Richard Rees, who has devoted so much care and thought to the task of making her comprehensible. His *A Sketch for a Portrait*, his editions of her letters and essays, and—his latest volume—*On Science, Necessity and the Love of God*, along with M. Gaboud's painstaking biography, provide a splendid documentation of her life and work. As my own first acquaintance with Simone Weil's writings—in my opinion, the most luminous intelligence of the twentieth century—is due to Sir Richard, I owe him a deep debt of gratitude for something that has, without exaggeration, intensified in a quite unique way the experience of living in the world today.

It is indeed a most extraordinary circumstance that a French Jewess who died tragically in her thirty-fifth year should have seen so deeply and so truly into the dilemmas of the Christian in our time. Yet so it is. Though she never was baptised she understood as few have the present relevance of Christ and the religion he founded. Her own private sufferings (she preferred the word 'affliction'), which were very great, gave her an exceptional insight into the nature of suffering and into the power of the cross both to express and to overcome it. One reads on, I find, with a kind of avid delight, leaping almost hilariously from sentence to sentence—like a man leaping from ice-floe to ice-floe on a swiftly flowing icy river.

Oddly enough, this applies even when her subject-matter—as in the case, so far as I am concerned, of her writings on abstruse scientific themes like the quantum theory and wave mechanics —is in itself beyond one's comprehension. As with certain musical compositions, there is, as it were, an outer envelope of incomprehensibility enclosing an inner core of clarity and lucidity. What emerges is a critique of science itself—for instance :

Everything that is most retrograde in the spirit of religion has taken refuge, above all in science itself. A science like ours, essentially closed to the layman, and therefore to scientists themselves, because each of them is a layman outside his own narrow specialism, is the proper theology of an ever increasingly bureaucratic society. 'It is secrecy, mystery, that is everywhere the soul of bureaucracy,' wrote Marx in his youth; and mystery is founded upon specialisation. Mystery is the condition of all privilege and consequently of all oppression; and it is in science itself, the breaker of idols, the destroyer of mystery, that mystery has found its last refuge.

Gravity, or necessity, Simone Weil argues, is the force pulling us and all creation down; from the sun is derived the energy enabling trees and us ourselves to stand and grow upright against this force. So the love of God, shining down like the sun, overcomes the downward pull of our earthiness. The same point is exquisitely made in her interpretation of the fairy story about the little tailor and the giant. They have a contest as to which of them can throw a stone farthest. The giant picks up a huge one and hurls it a prodigious height and a prodigious distance, but the little tailor releases a bird from his hand which flies away and is soon lost to view. Whatever is moved by power, or the will, that is to say, however terrific the force generated, must sometime, somewhere, fall to the ground, whereas whatever is animated by the spirit, or the imagination, can soar away like a bird high above the earth and into the sky.

The love of God and affliction are themes to which Simone Weil constantly returns. She sees affliction as a nail driven into our souls fastening us to the very centre of the universe—the 'true centre which is not in the middle, which is not in space and time, which is God.' So fastened, we are at 'the point of intersection between creation and Creator,' which is also the point of intersection of the two branches of the cross. When thought is confronted with affliction, she goes on, 'it takes immediate refuge in lies, like a hunted animal dashing for cover.' To deal with affliction, therefore, we have to go beyond thought and beyond the self, into the realm of Christ who conquered the world simply because he, being the Truth, continued to be the Truth in the very depth of extreme affliction.'

In other words, affliction, which to our mortal eye is intolerable and even ridiculous, is the way—and the only way—to understanding and being fully alive, and, what is more, to being able to help the afflicted. It is the commonest complaint today that affliction disproves the existence of a loving deity. Those terrible doctors I met on a television programme with Dr Christian Barnard laughed derisively when I spoke of man being made in the image of God. What an image! What a God! they jeered, thinking of the fearful things they had to see and cut away with their knives. Yet Simone Weil would say, as I consider justly, that not only does affliction not disprove God's existence—it uniquely manifests his presence. If every affliction were to be eliminated from our mortal existence then, and then only, God really would be dead.

Simone Weil's grasp and love of the Christian faith unfolded for her gradually, though there were definite stages. One was when, through a chance encounter with an English student in France, she read George Herbert's exquisite lines beginning: 'Love bade me welcome but my soul drew back.' In a splendid letter to Father Perrin (included in *Waiting on God*), she explains with great force and cogency why she cannot accept baptism. The document is balm indeed in the smoky, asphyxiating atmosphere of Christian consensus. As far as Simone Weil herself was concerned, through all her subsequent vicissitudes what happened when she read the Herbert lines—as she put it, Christ came down and took possession of her—was, she never doubted, for ever.

She is not easy to translate, the sense is so tight-packed, but Sir Richard Rees manages it excellently. He is himself so closely akin to her temperament and way of thought that he makes a perfect, if self-effacing, expounder and commentator. For me, at any rate, she emerges very clearly as a person. I think of her when I walk by the old Free French offices in London where she worked and I sometimes visited in the war years, and in Ashford where she is buried, having starved herself to death because she could not bring herself to eat more than the rations available in France. A suicide, the coroner said; an affliction in her own sense, rather, and, as with Bonhoeffer, a beginning not an end.

Observer, 22 September 1968

4. TOLSTOY

From childhood Tolstoy has seemed to me the greatest figure of modern times, and still does. I see him as one of those extraordinary beings in whom the conflicts of an age work themselves out. In this sense, his own life is his greatest production—more so even than his supreme masterpieces like *War and Peace, Anna Karenina* and *Resurrection*. Its interest is inexhaustible. If a new biography or study of him appeared annually I should still want to read them all. There have not been quite as many as that, but still a great many; in the latest one—by Henri Troyat—the bibliography contains seven pages of biographies and related studies, and, as is explained, the list is by no means complete.

M. Troyat's own biography (following his excellent Dostoevsky) is ample, and to the best of my knowledge complete. He is himself of Russian origin, and so can get inside Tolstoy's skin. The available documentation is in any case fabulous. All the Tolstoys were great diary-keepers. I have often amused myself by imagining the scene after lights-out at Yasnaya Polyana, when surreptitious candles were lit and notebooks brought out to record the impressions of the day's events, visitors and quarrels; then, as the night wore on, the padding about in stockinged feet to take a clandestine peep at one another's versions. Tolstoy himself kept a, supposedly, really secret diary which was hidden away; in his, as it were, open one he often used to carry on his disputes and quarrels with his wife, Sonya, who, he well knew, was bound to take a look at it sooner or later.

Probably no marriage in history has been so fully documented as the Tolstoys'; we know everything about it—down to the minutiae of their sexual relations. It certainly cannot be described as happy, but it went on for a long time and produced a large progeny. As M. Troyat shows, Tolstoy and Sonya clashed at every point. She was considerably younger than he was, decidedly conventional (though she thought otherwise) and a member in good standing of the Russian Orthodox Church. Tolstoy's ways and attitudes were utterly his own, without reference to anyone else or any outside considerations. The more passionate his Christian faith became the more he loathed the Church—a by no means unusual situation—and the more its dignitaries loathed him.

Poor Sonya hated his friends, particularly the humourless, pompous Chertkov, who I must say does seem to have been a pain in the neck. On one occasion he recorded: 'Tolstoy has learnt to ride a bicycle,' adding 'is this not inconsistent with his ideals?' On another, Tolstoy noticed a mosquito on Chertkov's bald pate and smacked at it with his hand. 'What have you done, Leo Nikolayevich?' Chertkov rebuked him, 'You have killed a living creature! You should be ashamed of yourself!'

Tolstoy, a deeply sensual man who at one period in his life abandoned himself to furious sexual indulgence, and remained to the end prone to what he called impure thoughts, became increasingly convinced that Christian salvation was attainable only if one died in the flesh to be reborn in the spirit. Sonya, understandably, found his abhorrence of his sexual appetites at the very least disconcerting, especially when, as was liable to happen, he was swept helplessly into frenzied indulgence of them with her. One has an impression in her diaries of the old fellow, after one such bout, rushing about their connubial bedroom tearing at his beard and crying: 'Woe! Woe!'

Deeply as I sympathise with Tolstoy's position, honesty compels me to recognise that it cannot have been much fun for the Countess, more particularly as the scene, thinly disguised but easily recognisable by all her friends, was quite likely to crop up in one of her husband's moralistic tales. In addition, his passion to identify himself completely with the muzhiks led him to give up bathing and attending to his person, with the result that his assaults on Sonya were often—to add to everything else—physically repugnant to her.

She herself complicated matters by developing a middle-aged passion for a rather foolish musician and frequent visitor to Yasnaya Polyana named Tanayev, with whom, to Tolstoy's intense disgust, she sometimes played duets. One should add that she got herself into so sick a state of mind one way and another that she came to accuse Tolstoy of homosexual relations with Chertkov—as unlikely a proposition, I should have said, as falling in love with a parking-meter.

There were also unending rows about money—in Tolstoy's view, next to sex the greatest single impediment to human

virtue and felicity. He was right, of course, but his own efforts
to rid himself of his possessions and live like the muzhiks were
constantly frustrated by the alleged needs of his family and
Sonya's championship of them. In the end, like King Lear, he
made over the inheritance to Sonya and the children, with disastrous consequences which may well, as George Orwell has
suggested, have induced him to take such fanatical exception to
that particular play of Shakespeare's, as well as to his work in
general.

Poor Tolstoy! He so desperately wanted to model his way of
life on the Sermon on the Mount, which embodied everything
he believed in and cared for on earth. And the harder he tried
the less adequately he seemed to succeed. Yet, after all, it was
the effort which counted—the effort and the vision. There was a
kind of grandeur in the very disparity between his aspirations
and his performance—in his fantastic vitality and exuberance, in
the glory of him; some relationship with life which made him,
at one and the same time, inextricably a part of life and yet
immeasurably above it and beyond it. Gorky put it best, perhaps
precisely because he did not share—in the Chertkov sense—all
Tolstoy's views:

> I know as well as others that no man is more worthy than he
> of the name of genius; more complicated, contradictory, and
> great in everything—yes, yes, in everything. Great—in some
> curious sense, indefinable by words—there is something in
> him which made me desire to cry aloud to everyone: 'Look
> what a wonderful man is living on earth.' For he is, so to say,
> universally and above all a man, a man of mankind.

Gorky's account of a glimpse he once caught of Tolstoy by
the sea is memorable—one of the best things of the kind I have
ever read:

> I once saw him as, perhaps, no one has ever seen him. I was
> walking over to him at Gaspra along the coast, and behind
> Yessupov's estate, on the shore among the stones, I saw his
> smallish angular figure in a grey, crumpled, ragged suit and
> crumpled hat. He was sitting with his head on his hands, the
> wind blowing the silvery hairs of his beard through his
> fingers; he was looking into the distance out to sea, and the

little greenish waves rolled up obediently to his feet and
fondled them as if they were telling something about themselves to the old magician. It was a day of sun and cloud, and
the shadows of the clouds glided over the stones, and with
the stones the old man grew now bright and now dark. The
boulders were large, riven by cracks, and covered with smelly
seaweed; there had been a high tide. He, too, seemed to me
like an old stone come to life, who knows all the beginnings
and the ends of things, who considers when and what will be
the end of the stone, of the grasses of the earth, of the waters
of the sea, and of the whole universe from the pebble to the
sun. And the sea is part of his soul, and everything around
him comes from him, out of him. In the musing motionless-
ness of the old man I felt something fateful, magical, something which went down into the darkness beneath him and
stretched up like a searchlight, into the blue emptiness above
the earth ... I cannot express in words what I felt rather
than thought at that moment; in my soul there was joy and
fear, and then everything blended in one happy thought: 'I
am not an orphan on the earth so long as this man lives on it.'

I feel the same because Tolstoy once did live on the earth. In
dealing with such a titan as Tolstoy, moral judgments in the
ordinary sense are absurd. Nor, again in the ordinary sense, can
one speak of tragedy, even in the case of his last crazy sortie
from Yasnaya Polyana and Sonya to die in the station-master's
little house at Astapovo, an obscure railway station on which,
while Tolstoy lingered there, the eyes of the whole world
rested. It all had the sort of aptness which eliminates tragedy—
the tragic grandeur and absurdity of life itself.

Observer, 10 March 1968

ME AND MYSELF

I saw you just now thumbing over a fat envelope of press cut-
tings with a glint in your eye. You jump on your mail with a
similar avidity—especially the fan letters, favourable or un-
favourable. How many hours you've spent in front of the
cameras, too, interviewing and being interviewed, airing your
views, holding forth! And yet you're always going on about
television and the media generally as a hateful exercise in collec-
tive and individual narcissism.

True: one's image (how I abominate that word!) is an inescapable preoccupation. I see the camera, far more than even
nuclear weapons, as the great destructive force of our time; it's
replaced the written and spoken word, captured the whole field
of art and literature. All the young want to do is to squint down
a tiny lens and see all the world in it; the only art they really
care about is celluloid. Yet how inferior and evanescent the
celluloid products are! Think of all the talent and money that's
been sunk in Hollywood, for instance—more, far more, than in
all the cities of Renaissance Italy. And the result in terms of
even minor art? Nil. When I think of all those miles and miles
of celluloid, from D. W. Griffith to Jean-Luc Godard . . .

How like you to go off into that tirade about the camera,
thereby evading the question of why you spent so much time in
front of it!

It began for me some fifteen years ago, when I was asked to
interview Billy Graham; I'd hardly even looked at television
before then, and hadn't the faintest notion of what it was going
to mean; to our way of life in general, and to me personally. It
was just something that turned up, and I did it, and went on
doing it.

Yes, but why?

For money, I suppose, and out of vanity. It's not particularly well paid, but one has the illusion that, compared with writing, it doesn't involve any work. Actually, it's very tiring and depressing. I don't think I've ever once walked off a television set without a feeling of despair. This is something to do with the medium itself, not any particular programme—though some, I admit, are more depressing than others. The worst I ever experienced—its horror abides with me still—was an encounter with Dr Christian Barnard and a studio full of distinguished doctors and surgeons. They were appalling in their grossness, their total inability to see beyond mortal flesh and their carving knives. By contrast, the most satisfying appearance I ever made was with Brendan Behan. This was because he was completely drunk; he just sat there, drunk and inviolate under the arc-lamps.

This doesn't explain why you go on appearing on television while perpetually denouncing the medium. Isn't that—to put it mildly—rather preposterous?

I see what you mean. I don't need the money any more, and at sixty-six vanity becomes ridiculous. Really, I don't think I've got much left. I have a sort of notion, though, that I may find an opportunity to say something, or convey something, which is worthwhile. Look at it this way. Supposing one was a pianist in a whore-house—one might be able to persuade oneself that occasionally including a hymn like 'Abide With Me' in one's repertoire would have a beneficial influence on the inmates. You see what I mean?

Yes, the more readily because you've used that comparison before.

So I have, and so would you if you had to write for a living. I agree it's not very convincing. It doesn't really convince me—which is why I can never bear to look at myself on television unless it's absolutely unavoidable. Whatever you put into it, what comes out is phoney—like a speech by Harold Wilson, or a National Theatre production. You've no idea how desolate it is on the other side of the cameras, how isolated one feels there, how cut off from reality—like a sea-lion washed up on Margate sands.

You've used that before, too.

I know I have, and I expect I'll use it again.

No doubt. What's all this about your being a Christian, and forgoing the pleasures of the flesh? I just can't tell you how sick I get of hearing you railing against the ills of a materialist society. You're just as greedy and randy as anybody else; rather more so, considering your years, I should have thought.

That might be true, but it doesn't alter the fact that a society like ours, dedicated to the pursuit of happiness, which means in practice the pursuit of pleasure—money, eroticism, success, etc., etc., with violence for kicks—is to me, very repellent. I'm entitled to express that opinion, I suppose?

Yes, you are, but not to go on expressing it.

Why not? You don't have to listen. It's my considered view that the way of life of Western man today is the most horrible and degraded that ever existed on earth . . .

Don't I know it? Oh, God, don't I know it?

. . . and what's more, it's breaking up so fast that, whereas I used to imagine it would somehow stagger on through my remaining years, I now think that these old eyes will see the crack-up. In a way, it's deliriously funny, of course—going to the moon when you can't walk with safety through Central Park, or for that matter through Hyde Park nowadays, after dark; fixing up a middle-aged dentist with a new heart in one part of Africa while in another part tens of thousands die of starvation in a squalid tribal war for which we, among others, provide the arms; promoting happiness enriched by an ever-rising Gross National Product, and sanctified by birth pills, pot and abortions for all on the National Health, while the psychiatric wards fill to overflowing, suicides multiply and crimes of violence increase year by year. I could go on and on.

I know you could, you often have, but please don't. What about your own behaviour? Don't you keep your head well down in the trough?

No, I don't, as a matter of fact, though my present abstemiousness, I admit, is a form of self-indulgence. It's something I like, that makes me happy. I should loathe nowadays to have my senses muddled or clouded by alcohol or drugs or tobacco, or even food. It's an exquisite pleasure to look out at life, as it were, through a window that isn't misted over; with the curtains drawn back and the light pouring in. All the persuasion to which one's subjected is, of course, in the opposite direction—to indulge one's appetites, particularly sexual ones. Advertising, current philosophical and even religious attitudes, aim at promoting the notion that satiety is the key to happiness and serenity. I don't agree. I think the Christian proposition is true—that we have to die in the flesh to be reborn in the spirit.

And I think you're just a sated old lecher who has reacted in the classic way by becoming an angry ascetic; a pinchbeck Savonarola, as someone called you. You pride yourself on an abstemiousness your past excesses have imposed on you, and, at the same time, out of rage and envy denounce the indulgence of others still fortunate enough to be young and in possession of their faculties.

My excesses, as you call them, weren't particularly pleasurable, and if you think I'm envious of the young today—well, think again. I pity them with all my heart, and perfectly understand their resort to aimless protest, dropping out, drugs and despair; sometimes to suicide. Nor is it true that my attitude has changed dramatically in old age. I always felt a stranger in the world, and for long have been sceptical about projects for improving our human lot. How little I've changed sometimes surprises me. For instance, the other day, looking over the four volumes of Orwelliana recently published, I came across a review he'd done of a book of mine (*The Thirties*) which I'd never seen before. My thesis, he wrote, 'boils down to a simple disbelief in the power of human beings to construct a perfect or even tolerable society here on earth. It is the Book of Ecclesiastes with the pious interpolations left out.' All that's happened subsequently (the review appeared in April 1940, when I was serving as a private in the army) is that I've put some of the pious interpolations back.

Incidentally, it was immensely moving to come across this review for the first time nearly thirty years after it was written. I could almost hear Orwell's rusty old voice speaking it. But forgive me. What else do you want to know?

What about money—which you affect to despise? You must be earning a lot nowadays.

I certainly earn a good deal more than I need. It would be absurd to earn less than I can, and the things I do for money for the most part I like doing. Otherwise, I shouldn't do them. So, I live modestly, try to behave generously—though not nearly generously enough—and comfort myself with the thought that my personal scale of living is not much, if at all, above that of, say, a retired schoolmaster. In any case, I'm convinced that money will shortly go down the drain; whatever we have we shall all lose—not over a course of years through slow inflation, but hey presto! and it'll be gone. My own little hoard—mainly derived from a paid-up insurance policy—will, I'm sure, disappear in this way. I could, of course, buy things with it now, which is what, as we all know, a lot of people are doing. As it happens, I don't want anything, so I just carry on. That's my situation.

I hear you, as Lord Reith would say, but somehow I'm not convinced.

Nor am I. About money and sex it's impossible to be truthful ever; one's ego is too involved. The only solution would be to become a lay-brother in a monastic order. Then one would have no stake in the world—no need to fight in its wars, grub for its money or grind out one's appetites at its behest and on its behalf. One would be free, in the same sort of way that, as Pasternak's hero in *Dr Zhivago* points out, under a Communist regime practically the only place where it's possible to be free is in prison. One has to be arrested to be free.

Why aren't you a lay-brother then?

Don't be silly. I've got a wife and children, and grandchildren, to my great delight. How could I be a monk? All I meant to say—as you perfectly understand—was that I often pined for total detachment from a society whose standards I despise and whose future prospects I regard as catastrophic, but in which I, none the less, have an inescapable stake.

Isn't that a rather pessimistic attitude?

To a shallow twentieth-century mind, yes. Actually, no. To suppose that our present way of life is viable, and that the trivial satisfactions it offers suffice to make us happy, would be pessi-

mistic indeed; to realise its wretchedness and inevitable break-
down, its fantasy and horror, is the height of optimism. The
darkness falls to idiot cries of progress achieved, of mankind
having come of age, with vistas of technological bliss, and a
Gadarene rush over the hills and far away. *Fiat nox!*

What a death-wisher!

On the contrary, as I come to realise this more clearly, I love
my fellow-men, the earth itself, the enchanting passage of time,
being alive, more, not less—something beyond your comprehension. All that has been achieved by our poor little human
species in the way of understanding and expounding what life is
about and how it works fills me with wonder and joy when I
see it in relation to the shining mystery of things; as scribble on
the fly-leaf of a mighty and incomprehensible tome. It's when
it's presented with infantile arrogance and credulity, as betoken-
ing men like gods, that it seems so pitiable and absurd.

*So you just fold your arms, convinced that there's nothing to
be done about anything. Isn't that Quietism?*

Or Jansenism. Or Manicheism. The prevailing notion is that
salvation can only come through action, and that whatever de-
flects our attention from here and now is an evasion, a selfish
pursuit of private virtue and serenity. Yet think of all the kingdoms of heaven on earth that have been proclaimed in our time.
Where are they now?—the Reich that was going to last a thousand years, Stalin's paradise so admired by Shaw and the
Webbs and all the other *illuminati* of the Left, the Welfare
State, the Great Society. The bottom's fallen out of all of them,
hasn't it? The trouble with kingdoms of heaven on earth is that
they're liable to come to pass, and then their fraudulence is
apparent for all to see. We need a kingdom of heaven in
Heaven, if only because it can't be realised.

*Perfect for those set in authority over us, isn't it? That's just
what they want to hear. They must love you nowadays!*

If so, they manage to hide it rather successfully. The great
illusion of the age is that truth consists of facts and virtue of
action. Actually, there's far more truth in the Book of Genesis
than in the quantum theory, and a Francis of Assisi or a Wesley
did far more to ameliorate the human condition than a

Beveridge or a Karl Marx. I've spent a number of years in India and Africa, where I found much righteous endeavour undertaken by Christians of all denominations; but I never, as it happens, came across a hospital or orphanage run by the Fabian Society or a Humanist leper colony.

So you discount all the efforts of the liberal-minded and progressive to make the world a better place and human life more tolerable?

Not precisely. I recognise that the motive is often admirable; unfortunately the result is almost invariably the exact opposite of what's intended. Thus, expanding public education has served to increase illiteracy; half a century of pacifist agitation has resulted in the two most ferocious and destructive wars of history, political egalitarianism has resulted in a heightened class-consciousness, and anti-capitalist legislation in intensified cupidity; internationalism has embittered the relations between nations, and sexual freedom has led to erotomania on a scale hitherto undreamed of. I could go on and on. Posterity (assuming there is one), is likely, in my opinion, to see liberalism and all its legislative and social consequences as the working-out of a collective death-wish. They will not otherwise be able to account for the fact that, in its name, the essentially Christian foundations of European civilisation were systematically undermined, its strength dissipated, and the moral, social and political order it had evolved irretrievably shattered. Public benevolence can never be a substitute for private virtue; it is more important, and more difficult, to check one outburst of temper, however trivial, than to engage in any number of public demonstrations against collective brutality and injustice.

Wouldn't it be more sensible, and more honest, then to go the whole hog and join the Roman Catholic Church?

There, again, speaks a contemporary mind. If not Moscow, Rome; if not humanism, deism; if not logical positivism, illogical negativism. I hate all the categories. The only thing I care about—dare I say it?—is truth, and its climate, love. There are a lot of things to admire in the Roman Catholic Church—its survival, its plainsong, its authentic internationalism, the tough, obstinate battle it has waged against the twentieth century;

above all, the fact that, with all its villainies and chicanery, it has managed to keep the allegiance of the poor. Leftist movements, whether led by a Stalin or a Harold Wilson, once they get into power are hated by the poor with particular virulence; the Protestant Churches have long ago become, like N.A.T.O., a headquarters without an army; the dissident students similarly have no rank and file. Yet still, before the altar-rail, the poor gather, opening their mouths hungrily for the Body and Blood of Christ. Not for much longer though, I think. The long resistance is over, the surrender about to take place—in the teeth of the opposition, let it be said to his eternal honour, of the present Pope. I used to suppose that the Roman Catholic Church, having so valiantly and obstinately defended its citadel against the assaults of a triumphant and vainglorious scientific materialism, would celebrate a well-deserved victory. Instead, to my amazement, just when the attacking forces were about to withdraw in disarray, the citadel's defenders have opened their gates and emerged bearing white flags.

That's for the telly. Render unto the telly the things that are the telly's. What we all want to know is what this sub-Chestertonian Christianity you're always blathering about nowadays means to you, if anything.

What does it mean to me?—a very bright light and very deep darkness, an inconceivable hope and blackest despair, an overwhelming love and an abysmal desolation; a man's life and death playing out the drama of the world, and the world's life and death playing out the drama of a man... But, look, the floor manager's signalling. Our time's up, I'm so sorry. It was so kind of you to come along to the studio this evening. Cut! Oh, Glory Alleluia, cut!

Observer, 15 December 1968

BY LAW ESTABLISHED

It is not by chance that the vogue word Establishment derives from the Church of England. With the monarch its titular head, and a largely pagan parliament responsible for its governance, this curious body has hitherto been one of the main props of the social and economic *status quo*. Nominally, it remains so still, but the actual support it offers proves on examination to be largely illusory, like one of those painted pillars one sees on Italian Renaissance buildings. Though the Archbishop of Canterbury may take precedence at ceremonial functions over other officers of the Crown like the Prime Minister, his effective authority, such as it is, scarcely reaches beyond the ramshackle institution over which he presides.

In matters like divorce, homosexuality and the so-called 'New Morality' the tide is flowing strongly against the traditional Christian position, often with the connivance of eminent churchmen. Witness the Archbishop's own attitude towards the Wolfenden report, abortion and divorce. Doctrinally and administratively the Church of England is in a parlous condition; liturgically, such disorder reigns that, with the best will in the world, one is hard put to it to decide whether one is attending Matins, Evensong, Holy Communion or some weird blend of all three begotten by the B.B.C. out of the Tractarian movement with Toc H intervening.

The simple fact is that, were the Church of England to be disestablished, it would infallibly fall flat on its face, revealing the inward decrepitude which the emoluments and trappings, the pomp and circumstance, derived from its nominal participation in the pageant of government, serve to disguise. It is not only in the rafters and pews of its edifices that dry rot and the death-watch beetle are at work; the whole body and structure of the Church are likewise in an advanced state of decay, which would immediately become apparent in the event of disestablishment. Ironically enough, today it is the Church's identification with the State, so often in the past a source of humiliation and despair to its best servants, that provides its only remaining strength.

The connection, in any case, is unlikely to be broken in the near or ascertainable future. A moribund Church and an ever more hedonistic civil power cling together, each one knowing he will collapse if he looses hold on the other. One may get a wry laugh out of the spectacle of parliamentarians resolutely refusing to countenance changes in a prayer book they have rarely had occasion to open; of Honourable and Right Honourable Members ardent for the Thirty-nine Articles embodying (as the Royal Warrant puts it) 'the true Doctrine of the Church of England agreeable to God's Word,' about which they know nothing, and care less, and which few of the bishops and clergy on whose behalf they are legislating any longer even pretend to believe, though all have solemnly assented to them to become ordained. A ribald scene indeed. Who would ever suppose that a secular enterprise so conducted could possibly thrive, or, for that matter, be permissible? Current professional, and even business, standards would preclude acceptance of a salaried post on the strength of a consciously fraudulent declaration. This, however, is the recognised practice among the Anglican clergy. Hilaire Belloc used to say that, when he considered the manner in which the Roman Church had been conducted, and by whom, he realised that it must have been divinely inspired to have survived at all. The saying applies with even greater force to the Church of England today; always assuming, of course, that in any real sense, it has survived.

Because of its identification with the State the Church could be relied on in times of crisis, like a war, or trouble over the matrimonial intentions of a recalcitrant monarch or princess, to rally to the side of those, as the Prayer Book puts it, set in authority over us. In the various wars of our time the Church has been insistent that God was on our side, and has given its unqualified blessing to whatever methods of waging them the generals and politicians might consider expedient. Even the annual party political conferences have thought fit to procure a benediction from the local vicar before settling down to the more serious business of jostling for position and devising appropriate electoral bribes and allurements.

If one were to pick on a single eminent ecclesiastic as marking the switch-over from supporting the traditional Establishment to looking benignly on the up-and-coming Leftist one, it would unquestionably be Archbishop William Temple. This burly prelate set a fashion, which has been assiduously copied, for translating hopes for a posthumous place in paradise into expectations that more comfortable and easy-going circumstances may be forthcoming in this world. Nothing, from the Church's point of view, could have been more disastrous. Who gets to heaven and what conditions are like there are matters about which the clergy can speak without fear of contradiction. By associating themselves with a prospectus for a kingdom of heaven on earth they, and their religion, were necessarily implicated when, as was inevitable, realisation proved disappointing. The trouble with earthly causes, however enlightened, is that they sometimes triumph. One of the wisest of the sayings of the founder of the Christian religion was that his kingdom was not of this world. Had he and his followers fallen into the snare of associating themselves with Jewish nationalism the Churches today, along with all their other worries, might have felt bound to offer a Christian defence of the State of Israel.

Since Temple's time Leftist clergymen have proliferated. A few, like the late Bishop Barnes of Birmingham and the former Dean of Canterbury, Dr Hewlett Johnson, have been rewarded with preferment in periods of Labour government; others, like the present Bishop of Southwark, Dr Mervyn Stockwood, have received their reward vicariously from Conservative administrations; yet others, like Canon Collins, have lent an air of clerical decorum to causes, like nuclear disarmament, which might otherwise be considered subversive and disreputable. Most, however, have had to content themselves with shocking their ever more minute and somnolent congregations, and with finding an outlet for their, as they hope and believe, explosive views in their parish magazines.

In such circumstances it is not surprising that the ministry should attract crackpots, eccentrics and oddities who in happier times would have appeared as characters in Waugh's earlier novels rather than as beneficed clergymen. Scarcely a day goes by but some buffoon in holy orders makes an exhibition of himself in one way or another, more often than not on the subject of sex—that *pons asinorum* of our time. Can it be wondered at, then, that the Church's voice, when heard, is more often than not greeted with derision or just ignored?

In an average English village today Anglican worship has become little more than a dying bourgeois cult. A small cluster of motor-cars may be seen outside the parish church when a service is in progress; the bells still ring joyously across the fields and meadows on Sunday mornings and evenings, but fewer and fewer heed them, and those few predominantly middle-class, female and elderly. It never occurs to most villagers that the Church is anything to do with them, apart from the need for baptism, marriage and burial; three ceremonies which continue for no particular discernible reason, to draw them to church.

It must be desperately disheartening, and the incumbent often gives the impression of being dispirited and forlorn. Whatever zeal he may have had as an ordinand soon gets dissipated in an atmosphere of domestic care and indifference on the part of his flock. Small wonder, then, that in the pulpit he has little to say except to repeat the old traditional clerical banalities, as invariable as jokes in *Punch*; sometimes, in deference to the twentieth century, lacing the sad brew with references to the United Nations, apartheid and the birth pill. He doubtless feels himself to be redundant. The villagers stoically die without his ministrations; they would resent any interruption of their evening telly if he ventured to make a call, and have for long accustomed themselves to cope, without benefit of clergy, with minor misfortunes like pregnancy and delinquency.

In the large cities the situation is not dissimilar. Only in the suburbs and new towns is there a drift back to the churches, though one may presume to wonder how far this is due to the sheer agonising boredom and emptiness of this particular way of life, and how far to an authentic spiritual awakening. In any case, such pockets of a revived interest in the Church scarcely offset the otherwise prevailing apathy. An ardent Christian evangelist remarked to me recently that, when he preaches the Gospel nowadays, he finds no hostility, still less any tendency to argue combatively; only total indifference and incomprehension.

Agnostics of my generation, whether consciously or not, were still part of a Christian history and tradition, which has coloured all their moral attitudes and assumptions. This is so no longer. The very language and terms of the Christian religion are incomprehensible to a generation which hears nothing about them at home, and for whom religious instruction at school consists more often than not of civics, sex or mental arithmetic. It is, perhaps, absurd to suppose that the Church of England in its present state, or, it may be, ever in its history, could measure up to so desperate a situation. It never has been much given to fervour, and has usually lost its zealots, like Newman and Wesley, to the Roman Church or Nonconformity. Moderation has been its watchword. I remember reading an eighteenth-century sermon which referred to the 'truly extraordinary behaviour of Judas Iscariot,' and there was the famous case of a bishop who allegedly remarked that the Ten Commandments were like an examination paper, with eight only to be attempted.

All this is not without its charm. Yet in existing circumstances such bizarre offerings are like a sweet liqueur to thirsty men. The thirst is very great; much greater and more widespread than is commonly supposed, as anyone who has dealt at all with religious matters on television must be aware. There is a conscious and passionate awareness that this morally appalling and spiritually impoverished affluent society in which we live, with its accent everlastingly on consumption and sensual indulgence of every kind, is no better than a pigsty. I know of no more satisfying statement of the case for lifting our snouts out of the trough than the words and music of Anglican worship. Alas, they sound hollowly today, intoned by dispirited priests in near-empty churches.

Daily Telegaph Magazine, 28 January 1966

HAPPINESS

The sister-in-law of a friend of Dr Johnson was imprudent enough once to claim in his presence that she was happy. He pounced on her hard, remarking in a loud, emphatic voice that if she was indeed the contented being she professed herself to be, then her life gave the lie to every research of humanity; for she was happy without health, without beauty, without money and without understanding. It was rough treatment, for which Johnson has been much criticised, though it should be remembered that he spoke as an eighteenth-century man, before our present preoccupation with happiness as an enduring condition of life became prevalent. Actually, I think I see his point.

There *is* something quite ridiculous, and even indecent, in an individual claiming to be happy. Still more, a people or a nation making such a claim. The pursuit of happiness, included along with life and liberty in the American Declaration of Independence as an inalienable right, is without any question the most fatuous which could possibly be undertaken. This lamentable phrase—the pursuit of happiness—is responsible for a good part of the ills and miseries of the modern world. To pursue happiness, individually or collectively, as a conscious aim is the surest way to miss it altogether; as is only too tragically evident in countries like Sweden and America where happiness has been most ardently pursued, and where the material circumstances usually considered conducive to happiness have been most effectively constructed. The Gadarene swine were doubtless in pursuit of happiness when they hurled themselves to destruction over the cliff. Today, the greater part of mankind, led by the technologically most advanced, are similarly bent, and if they persist, will assuredly meet a similar fate. The pursuit of happiness, in any case, soon resolves itself into the pursuit of pleasure, something quite different—a mirage of happiness, a false vision of shade and refreshment seen across parched sand.

Where, then, does happiness lie? In forgetfulness, not indulgence, of the self. In escape from sensual appetites, not in their satisfaction. We live in a dark, self-enclosed prison which is all we see or know if our glance is fixed ever downwards. To lift it upwards, becoming aware of the wide, luminous universe outside—this alone is happiness. At its highest level such happiness is the ecstasy which mystics have inadequately described. At more humdrum levels it is human love; the delights and beauties of our dear earth, its colours and shapes and sounds; the enchantment of understanding and laughing, and all other exercise of such faculties as we possess; the marvel of the meaning of everything, fitfully glimpsed, inadequately expounded, but ever-present.

Such is happiness—not compressible into a pill; not translatable into a sensation; lost to whoever would grasp it to himself alone, not to be gorged out of a trough, or torn out of another's body, or paid into a bank, or driven along a motorway, or fired in gun-salutes, or discovered in the stratosphere. Existing, intangible, in every true response to life, and absent in every false one. Propounded through the centuries in every noteworthy word and thought and deed. Expressed in art and literature and music; in vast cathedrals and tiny melodies; in everything that is harmonious, and in the unending heroism of imperfect men reaching after perfection.

When Pastor Bonhoeffer was taken off by his Nazi guards to be executed, as I have read, his face was shining with happiness, to the point that even those poor clowns noted it. In that place of darkest evil, he was the happiest man—he, the executed. I find this an image of supreme happiness.

B.B.C. broadcast, 5 October 1965

CONSENSIANITY

A visit to the World Council of Churches at Uppsala in Sweden confirmed my feeling that institutional Christianity is quietly but inexorably extinguishing itself. Ecumenicalism is predominantly, I should suppose, a response to this sense of being about to become extinct, rather than to any zeal for union as such. The most vital elements in the Christian story have, in any case, derived from dissidence rather than agreement—St Francis, Ignatius Loyola, Luther, Pascal, Wesley, Kierkegaard, etc., etc. At Uppsala, as one clearly saw, they were able to agree about almost anything because they believed almost nothing. They reminded me of a pub turn-out in my youth, with ten or a dozen drunks holding on to one another, swaying to and fro, but managing to remain upright. Alone, they would infallibly have fallen into the gutter. It was all tremendously reminiscent of the United Nations, that tragically absurd assembly—stony faces between earphones, paper circulating in prodigious quantities (the Swedish Government allotted ten tons, which got used up in the first two days), oratory to match, interminable discussions about the precise wording of statements of belief and purpose which few would read and none heed, a well-equipped but little-used press room, documents of no conceivable importance or interest to anyone urgently rushed out to choke the pigeon-holes of absent journalists.

If ever in human history there was a non-event, this was it. I cannot see how, apart from the desultory use of the cross as a symbol and the garb of some of the delegates, anyone could possibly have known that the occasion had anything to do with the Christian religion. The natural assumption would have been that it was an assembly of the well-intentioned concerned to deal with some of the world's problems like hunger and racialism, but displaying little clear notion of how to set about it, and anyway disposing of no authority or resources commensurate with the task.

It is natural enough, I suppose, that the Churches in their final decrepitude should thus concentrate on their social, and ignore their spiritual, responsibilities. Thereby they fall in with the prevailing temper of the age; everyone can understand the merit of giving a starving man food, or of championing the victims of napalm or apartheid, but the very language of mysticism or transcendentalism has ceased to be comprehensible. In St Augustine's *Confessions* I read: 'I no longer hoped for a better world because I was thinking of the whole of creation, and in the light of this clearer discernment I had come to see that though the higher things are better than the lower, the sum of all creation is better than the higher things alone.' The Churches, on the contrary, feel bound to proclaim a better world, thereby promoting their own extinction. For if a better world were attainable, they would be unnecessary; if—as is far more probable—it is unattainable, they cannot but be involved in the consequent disillusionment.

Their better world promotion has the short-term advantage of being a soft sell. How much easier, and even pleasurable, to march to the American Embassy to protest against the war in Vietnam than to march to Gethsemane! Even the saints have found Christian virtue hard to practise, but any tousled student can acquire a glow of righteousness by pouring a bucket of paint over some visiting speaker from the U.S. Embassy or South Africa House. And how many of those who so ardently collect for Oxfam reflect that if the amount collected were multiplied by a thousand it would still not come anywhere near compensating for those Indian doctors who keep our (on Asian standards) over-manned Health Service going? Again, many more people are killed and injured on the world's roads any bright week-end than in a month of the Vietnam war, but whoever heard of a protest march about that? To stop the slaughter on the roads it would be necessary to restrict motoring, which the Churches could not possibly recommend. It would amount to restricting pleasure, which, in terms of the pursuit of happiness, is the ultimate abomination. In a materialist society, pleasure alone is sacred, and its instruments (money, contraceptives, drugs, etc.) are invested with sanctity and regarded with veneration—the modern equivalent of the bones of St Peter or fragments of the True Cross.

One of the few sensible observations came from the Russian Orthodox Metropolitan, Nicodim of Leningrad and Novgorod. 'How', he asked, 'can there be a dialogue of Christians and Marxists when between them there is an insuperable abyss, and when the basic beliefs of the one are denied by the other?' This bearded, youthful prelate, I reflected, has to deal with the most brutally tyrannical and materialistic regime the world has yet known, unlike these soft confused upholders of the Protestant Establishment drivelling away their lives in pursuit of a phantom kingdom of heaven on earth. To him, therefore, the full absurdity of trying to marry the ideas of Marx and Christ is all too apparent. Metropolitan Nicodim has to take his orders from the Kremlin bosses, certainly, but at least he is under no necessity to pretend that they and he pursue the same ends. In the Americanised part of the world, on the other hand, the situation is far worse. There the Churches joyously accept the Devil's offer of the kingdom of heaven on earth, with, of course, the subsequent commitment to fall down and worship him.

The collector's item in the output of the World Council of Churches was a paper entitled 'Towards a New Style of Living' —the nearest the Council got to grappling with the Christian notion of being reborn. Except a man find a new style of living, instead of: *Except a man be born again*. The paper contains a priceless collection of current cant:

... a creation stirred to newness by scientific and technical inventions ... generations are finding it increasingly difficult to communicate ... young people ... experimenting with new styles of life ... marching, popular music, sit-ins, mural newspapers, hippies and imaginative dress ... in all relations between men and women there is always a sexual component ... too often chastity is thought of simply in terms of abstinence or of keeping intercourse within marriage ... an essential link between healthy sexuality and personal fulfilment ...

I appreciate very much, too, the sweeping McLuhanesque generalisations like 'The contemporary world is dominated by middle-class people, the majority of whom are white Europeans and North Americans.' For a moment it pulls you up. The U.S.S.R. and China dominated by white middle-class Europeans and North Americans! Can it be? India, too, and Indonesia, and all those liberated African territories ruled over by Jomo and Hastings and Julius and Kenneth and Apollo Milton! Are they all white middle-class Europeans and North Americans? But back to the text:

... Christians of all age brackets should join with people of all convictions in providing opportunities for the generations to grow together ... secular technological civilisation which is spreading over the world ... reconciliation which means directing conflicts towards constructive ends ... discernment of appropriate forms of living ...

And so on. All very soothing and reassuring I suppose, if you like that kind of thing, but scarcely in the vein of St Paul.

By travelling the thirty miles into Stockholm the Uppsala delegates could see a new style of living for themselves, there examine, if they so fancied, some of its embellishments—for instance, eye over the lavish piles of pornography in the bookshops, or slip in surreptitiously to take a look at the sexual act portrayed in full on film (*I am Curious Yellow*). A young Swede explained to me that the film is socially significant in that the heroine, bicycling from one sexual encounter to another, is seated on a box labelled 'Social Conscience.' This theme, which a Hogarth or a Gillray would have handled so perfectly, well symbolises, I decided, the World Council of Churches—the little label of social virtue carrying so heavy a load of personal sin. How splendidly appropriate, how superb an example of what Blake calls 'fearful symmetry,' that the largest ever gathering of the legatees of a bankrupt Christendom should take place in a leaden Scandinavian paradise, with all those sad, earnest faces going sadly and earnestly about their pleasures.

A DIALOGUE WITH ROY TREVIVIAN

R.T. Malcolm, can you tell me first of all where were the seeds of religion planted in you? Were you brought up in a religious home? Was your childhood in any way surrounded by the idea of God?

M.M. It is very difficult to know exactly what a religious home is. Let me tell you about my home. My father was a pioneer Socialist and Fabian, and if he had a religion that was it. We were brought up to regard Socialism as the one thing that mattered, and it is quite arguable that my very strong reaction against the idea of creating a kingdom of heaven on earth may be a sort of reaction to this, exactly as many people brought up in, say, a strongly Methodist home react the other way. But, of course, my father, like so many of the early Socialists, and in my opinion, the best, was a spill-over from the Chapel. He was a very poor boy; he left school when he was thirteen, and he told me once when he was quite old, and I never forgot it, that from the age of thirteen there were always other people dependent upon him. Well, the Chapel was everything. The Chapel was his university. He went to Mock Parliaments, literary societies and terrible things called Mutual Improvement societies. His Socialism was derived from such activities as these. So he had a sort of Christian background, which I certainly absorbed.

R.T. You mean he expressed this form of Christianity in the home?

M.M. He expressed it in the sense that we were brought up to revere the person of Christ, but we were also brought up to ridicule the Church and dogmas of all kinds, including the Crucifixion. My father often spoke at meetings, and I followed him round even when I was very young. He

would sometimes speak at religious meetings, always refer-
ring the Christian gospel to his notions of a better world
and a better society. That was the religion in which I was
brought up and which I accepted.

R.T. But did it include going to Church?

M.M. I did in fact go for a time to a Congregational Church,
though primarily, I confess, for social reasons; specifically
for the mundane purpose of meeting girls. This may
seem strange in the light of the present situation. We were
a family of boys, and we never knew any girls, and one
of the few occasions when I met girls in a vaguely romantic
way was at Chapel. Also there was a rather marvellous old
clergyman there, a Congregational minister, a Scotsman
called Sanderson. I can see him now—a remarkable old
chap with a long white beard, who used to talk about the
New Testament in a vivid and picturesque way, especially
about fishermen. Having come from the Shetland Islands
he knew a lot about fishermen, and he would bring to his
exposition of the New Testament a knowledge of fishermen which appealed to me very much. But that was not
a very deep impression. I can also trace in myself, when I
look back, another strain, and that was a feeling I always
had as a child, and have now, of being a stranger in this
world; of not being a native. I can remember it so vividly,
as almost the first recollection of life—an overpowering
feeling that this world is not a place where I really belong.

R.T. When you say this world, do you mean the universe, or
do you mean the way man is in the universe?

M.M. I mean my physical existence in time. I couldn't have put
it that way then, but I know the inconceivable poignancy
with which I first heard the phrase in the Bible 'a stranger
in a strange land'. I don't think any phrase I have ever
heard gave me such a sense of poignancy.

R.T. Can you fill this out a little bit more so that I can understand clearly what you mean?

M.M. It's not easy because this is, I think now, the essence of
mysticism and of a mystical view of life—this sense that
man has of not completely belonging here. He doesn't

belong here because his soul belongs to eternity, whereas this is a place of time and bodies. It is the feeling out of which all art, all literature, all mystical concepts, all philosophy, anything like that, has come.

R.T. When did this feeling first come to you?

M.M. I tell you in all honesty, almost the first thing I can remember as a conscious child was this feeling that somehow or another I didn't belong here; that here is not my home. It was only afterwards when I began to read writers like Blake and Pascal, the writers that I now think are the great luminaries of modern times—also Tolstoy—that I understood the relation between mysticism and feeling a stranger in a strange land. All this business of men's alienation, which is on every tongue now, seems to me to relate directly to this feeling of not belonging here. If I could point to one single basic feeling out of which the structure of my mind and thought and belief grew, it would be this—that I do not belong here.

R.T. As a young person, did this feeling of estrangement in the world go hand in hand with a feeling that God loved you?

M.M. Not till much later, because God didn't arise in my upbringing. But it did mean—and I have to make this clear immediately—that all the worldly things, essential things, like money and fame and success and sensuality, which even a child is aware of, even though I was greedy for them, decidedly so, perhaps even above the average, I never really liked them, I never thought they were any good.

R.T. And yet at quite a young age you threw yourself wholeheartedly into supporting the Socialist movement.

M.M. Oh, very strongly so—absolutely. But that was partly just love of my father. He was a most delightful man, and I loved him dearly. I not only loved him, but I completely accepted his view of the world. I was absolutely convinced that if my father and his friends took over, which I firmly believed they would, because it all seemed to me to be so reasonable what they said, that everything was going to be fine. It was just a matter of time, and people would see that the capitalist system was useless; that everybody should stay at school until they were sixteen or seventeen, and that leisure time should be devoted to reading Shakespeare instead of going to race meetings, and so on and so on. All this seemed to me to be obvious, and it was just a matter of my father and his friends winning votes and getting into power. The whole thing was as clear as day.

R.T. Where does your mother figure in all this?

M.M. My mother played a very small part in my life strangely enough. She was a terribly nice woman, straight working-class, whereas my father belonged to the lower middle class. His father was an undertaker who disappeared very early on, and his mother started a second-hand furniture business in Penge, but it was all in terms of the lower, lower middle class. My mother's family lived in Sheffield, in back-to-back houses, and were all steel-workers. My father met her in the Isle of Man when he was on holiday. It was a sort of H. G. Wells episode—he a young clerk holidaying in the Isle of Man, and she a girl from Sheffield, very pretty, very pretty indeed, and he fell in love with her and brought her south. When we used to go and visit her family, whom we adored, the funny thing to me is, looking back, that theoretically, of course, they were the down-trodden and oppressed and we were the up-and-coming, but in actual terms of standard of life, we children always considered that we had a much better 'blow out' with them, and that their house was warmer and their whole manner of life more lavish than ours—which it was, as a matter of fact, because they spent everything on these comforts.

R.T. A big fire and plenty of food on the table . . .

M.M. Absolutely—and of course in Yorkshire that meant plenty of home-made food of a very high order of excellence. For instance, at Christmas we would be fairly certain a hamper would come to us from Sheffield full of delicacies. Like so many lower middle-class families with their belief in education and all that sort of thing, we lived really very abstemiously, relative to the working classes who didn't give a damn about all that, but just wanted to be comfortable. And comfortable they were in those days.

R.T. Your mother still seems very much a ghostlike figure. You didn't have very much to do with her?

M.M. She wasn't exactly ghostlike, but she was utterly uneducated; she could barely write—I don't mean that she was a fool by any manner of means, but she could barely write, and all my passionate interest in life was centred on books. My father was really a very extraordinary man, and having left school at thirteen he taught himself French, and was very well read. He even taught himself to play the piano. He had a passion for learning that men of that type had. He went up to London at about eight o'clock from East Croydon station, and he would return at about six o'clock; he would then engage in several hours of municipal activity because he was a town-councillor—committees, meetings. And on top of all that (and how the hell did he do it? one now asks onself) he would educate himself, and continued to do so until the day of his death —to read and to think and to make notes. I have got one of his notebooks. On Saturday afternoon, which was his afternoon off, he would maybe go off and bicycle from Croydon to Tunbridge Wells and address a meeting, and then bicycle back. He had fantastic energy, and all my interest was centred on him.

R.T. What did your mother contribute, then?

M.M. She kept the house going, she washed and cleaned and cooked; we had no help of any kind.

R.T. Did she understand you?

M.M. No, not at all. I never had a conversation of mutual understanding with my mother at all. I used to read my father's books precociously, and she once found me reading Rousseau's *Confessions*, when, God knows, I must have been very young. I shouldn't think I knew what it was about really, but she gave me a frightful dressing down, and said that Rousseau was a bad man. I remember the phrase she used, very typical; she said 'Rousseau was born with his blood boiling.' I had no idea what she meant by this, but I realise now that it was a sort of primitive way of saying that he was sexually obsessed.

R.T. We both know enough about Freud for me to be able to ask : Could not this feeling of estrangement in the universe be due to the lack of a strong link with your mother?

M.M. It could be so, but I think if it were, then all the Christian mystics would have had mothers from whom they were alienated—which is very much not the case. Take, for instance, the case of St Augustine, who is a very sympathetic figure to me. His mother was a colossally strong influence on his life. I am exceedingly doubtful about all that psychological stuff, and I don't really believe in it at all. I think Freud produced one of the worst sort of grotesque over-simplifications. After all, what he hit on was very simple and obvious—that sex, the procreative urge, is a basic urge, which can't be left out of account. Well, that's perfectly obvious, and it probably had been left out of account, but I think it now is taken too much into account. It has sometimes occurred to me that Freud and Marx were two Jews who punished us for all we had done to the Jews by, in effect, destroying the Christian religion. Freud destroyed it by taking away any sense of personal responsibility for wrongdoing.

R.T. I don't go along with you in what you say about being a stranger here. I would say that here I have no continuing dwelling-place, but I feel at home in the universe. I feel that it is a friendly place, I don't think that I am alienated from the universe.

M.M. I love it. I love it. Every day I live in the world I love it more. Every time I look out of that window, I love it, every leaf, every colour, and the more I feel myself a stranger the more I love it. Because I know that the whole of this has a much larger dimension than my eye can pick out.

R.T. I see, you don't feel *alienated* from the *universe*?

M.M. I feel only that I don't live here. I am visiting.

R.T. Oh yes, yes, but you can feel at home here?

M.M. Yes, I am having a delightful time, but I'm making a brief visit, and therefore all plans that are based on the idea that we live permanently here, and that this is the beginning and end of life, seem to me ludicrous.

R.T. When did this business about religion and the possible truth of what Jesus Christ was teaching, when did this come back to you in a big way?

M.M. I don't think there was ever a dramatic moment when it came back. I have often thought about this. It's something —well, put it this way—it has always seemed to me that the most interesting thing in the world is to try and understand what life is about. This is the only pursuit that could possibly engage a serious person—what is life about? And of course it is a continuing pursuit. As I have realised the fallacy of all materialist philosophies and materialist utopias, and of the politics of utopianism, so I have come to feel more and more strongly that the answer to life does not lie in materialism. In seeking the other transcendental answer I have inevitably and increasingly been driven to the conclusion, almost against my own will, that for a West European whose life and background and tradition are in terms of Western European Christian civilisation, the only answer lies in the person and life and teaching of Christ. Here, and here only, the transcendental answer is expressed adequately and appropriately. Now that is not the kind of conclusion that involves anything like a Damascus Road experience. It is a process of continuing realisation. On the other hand, of course, one reaches a point when one comes out into the open about it. For me that was delayed because I felt it was necessary that my personal life should not be a disgrace to the Christian religion when I avowed it. There were certain things which I had to do about my personal life. In my particular case—and I am not laying this down as any kind of a rule—this involved abstemiousness and asceticism, and the mastery of self-indulgence.

R.T. Can you give me some instances?

M.M. The most trivial ones are drinking and smoking, both of which I indulged in fairly lavishly. These are obvious enough, as is over-eating. The most important of all is sex—I mean indulgence in promiscuity. That is more difficult because sex is, of all forms of self-indulgence, the one which makes the most appeal to the imagination. Greed, cupidity and related pursuits are really rather vulgar and make very little appeal to the imagination. But sexual indulgence makes a considerable appeal. Therefore, it is the hardest to conquer, but in my opinion it is absolutely essential that it should be conquered.

R.T. You are saying to me that before you could avow that you were a Christian these things had to be renounced.

M.M. Yes. I felt very strongly that I couldn't take on something for which I had such a respect as I have for the Christian religion if I was liable to disgrace it. I believe that no moral proposition is worth propounding unless it is also expressed in terms of personal conduct. If I say that all men are my brothers, the first thing I have to be sure of is that I do veritably feel them to be so, and behave accordingly. If I don't, better not to say it.

R.T. And act on it.

M.M. And act on it. If I don't do that, better keep quiet. Thus, for instance, in the case of the racial problem in the United States, I feel in many ways more comfortable about it in the Southern States than in the North, because in the South the arrangement which prevails, vicious though it is, at least expresses the actual state of mind of people, and is therefore more bearable. Moral propositions without action are as sick as sex without procreation. That's precisely what's wrong with liberalism—the basic ideology of our society. So it seems to me that all moral feelings that one might have, and all moral propositions one might wish to propound, must be related to personal conduct. If you take the basic Christian view of life that one must die in the flesh in order to be reborn—then one must be master of one's flesh, and it is quite impossible to combine that with self-indulgence, especially sexual self-indulgence, whether outside or inside matrimony. I think it is also a base thing to seek to perpetuate sex once the actual urge is passed. So all this had to be dealt with. For me it was like a man who wanted to apply to join a particular club or, better, religious order. First of all he had to be sure that he could fulfil the requirements. That took me a certain amount of time and effort. It would be very wicked of any man to say that he had completely achieved mastery of his fleshly appetites, but I felt able to declare myself a Christian when I was reasonably sure that a scrutiny of my life would not disgrace the inconceivably high standards that Christians I admire—like Tolstoy and Pascal—have set.

R.T.   But what about fame? You have more fame now than you ever had. Isn't this a form of indulgence?

M.M.   I suppose it would be if one cared much about it, but I don't. I think I am being genuine. I don't say that occasionally, if I know that people are aware of me, there isn't a sort of satisfaction—but there is also a sort of dissatisfaction. If tomorrow such fame as I enjoy were to be completely obliterated, it wouldn't worry me; it wouldn't worry me at all, it wouldn't cost me a pang. But I agree, of course, that it is a thing you have to watch, because one's ego is indestructible, and the devil is always there working on this ego. The old-fashioned idea that there is a force in us of wickedness which is the Devil, is, in my opinion, completely true. And of course, the ego, the Devil's instrument, is always there to his hand. But fame is not a thing to which I attach much value; neither to fame nor to money. I attach perhaps excessive value to being good at my chosen work—which is writing or communicating. If someone says to me: 'That was a marvellous thing you wrote,' or, 'I was enormously impressed by what you said,' this gives me a glow of pleasure, and I don't think a wholly unworthy one because, although it is connected with vanity, the pleasure in it is more, I hope and believe, the sense that one has communicated something to someone which was worthy. You know that marvellous saying of Christ's, 'Let your light shine';

well, when one feels that one has shone a little light, that is what gives satisfaction. I should still like to stress that I do not believe in asceticism for asceticism's own sake. In other words, I am not a Puritan in any sense. I don't think there is virtue in self-denial as such. If I want to do something, and I stop myself doing it, I don't think that is virtuous, though it may be wise or well-advised. For myself, personally, I have found that I can only concentrate my thoughts and activities on Christianity and everything connected with it—which is the one object I care about in life now—if I don't indulge my senses. This applies even to over-eating, which is quite a harmless thing.

R.T. What do you mean when you say over-eating?

M.M. I simply mean eating a lot. Actually, I am a vegetarian nowadays and eat rather little. If I eat a lot, still more if I drink a lot, or smoke a lot, or indulge in sexual activities a lot, this means to me personally, with my sort of make-up, that I am shut off from the sight of God. The image which I use to myself is taken from driving. If it's too hot inside the car, if the temperatures outside and inside are ill-adjusted, then the windscreen mists over and and you can't see. In the same sort of way, if I allow myself to become preoccupied with my bodily appetites, my soul's window gets misted over and I can't see out. I do not in any way criticise people who don't feel similarly. I do not think that abstinence is essential to the pursuit of truth through Christianity, though I notice that the figures in the past whom I most admire, and whose writings and thoughts most appeal to me, usually did take that way. So there must be some connection. Even so, I would never preach abstinence to people as such; I would point out to them that my experience of life, such as it is, suggests that an integral part of looking at the spiritual reality of life is divorcing yourself as far as possible from involvement in the sensual or physical part. I make one exception to that. For me, in my life, there has been only one sensual experience which has carried spiritual undertones, and that is the ecstasy of physical passion when one is young and when it is associated with love. That is an experience which has, I think, spiritual undertones. It explains why in literature it is the only sensual passion which has produced great art. Other forms of indulgence have not; they have produced oddities of writing, or perversions of writing, but they have not produced great literature. That particular experience has, and it is the one exception. But I would emphasise the point that it belongs to youth, and that efforts to protract it and to apply it in middle age or old age usually produce horror and distortion. Money as a pursuit is, in my opinion, about the most contemptible of all. On the other hand we need money to live, and I don't think as a factor in life it is in itself either good or bad. After all, it is only a means of exchange. I have never pursued money; most of my life I have been relatively poor. In the years before the 1939–45 war, as a free-lance writer, I seldom earned as much as £20 a week. That, with a wife and four children, was certainly not affluence. Yet it is a time I look back on with great satisfaction. I think that people who are poor and have to live modestly and bring up children at considerable sacrifice to themselves are fortunate, not unfortunate. It is the others who are unfortunate. They are missing out on something very exhilarating and delightful.

R.T. Can you develop that a little bit?

M.M. Judging from my own friends and people that I have known, those who escape these difficulties miss a great deal. Christians are often accused of being morbid when they talk of the joy of sacrificing. I think it is one of the deepest truths of the Christian religion. Far from being a source of sadness, sacrifice is a great joy and source of illumination—perhaps the greatest of all. I also think that to live modestly is always a richer experience, because you are living like the majority of people; the trouble with the rich, as I have known them, is not really that they are bad people, but that they are cut off from an essential experience they don't understand. For ninety-nine per cent of human beings their lives are governed by the struggle to acquire the means to live. This is how the arrangement is, and if you don't experience that you miss a great deal. I don't think I ever had a bank pass-book in black until I was well into my forties. With four children there were always unexpected expenses, and so one was always in the red.

R.T. Did this make you anxious?

M.M. I have been anxious about money, yes, and I think the bad side of poverty is the fear that it creates, but I would certainly think that the unreality of life for the rich, and ultimately the boredom of life for them, is a worse misfortune. Lately I have earned a lot, and I have had to confront the question of what I should do about it, Here again abstemiousness is a help. At least I can say that expenditure on myself is now minimal. The idea of a big house, servants, that sort of thing, would be in any case abhorrent; my own present personal scale of living is certainly no higher than it would be if I had retired on a small pension. This seems to me preferable to falling into the sort of ethical and financial shifts that Tolstoy's efforts to have no property or earnings at all involved. At the same time, of course, I have to recognise that whatever financial stringency I have known in the past, it has never been at all comparable with the grinding poverty which, to our shame, continues to exist in the affluent societies of America and Western Europe; still less with the ever worsening poverty of Africa and Asia. Nor, I know, is my way of life, however abstemious, other than privileged by comparison with the great majority of my fellow-men. I often wish it were otherwise; the only uniform I have ever looked at with envy is that of a lay-brother. A phrase used by St Francis of Assisi that I once read has continued to echo in my mind—'naked on the naked earth.' So placed, even in this cruel and unjust world, one could live and sleep in peace.

R.T. Asceticism, as you have described it to me, is not an end in itself, but is a means of clearing the way for a deeper

communion with God. Malcolm, what do you imagine
about God? I know this is a ridiculous and impossible
question, but up to not long ago people had an image of
God, and then we were told we mustn't have images of
God, that God was the ground of our being, God wasn't
out there, God was in here, and so on. I find it almost
impossible to pray to God, talk about God, imagine God,
without imagining something. I would like you, if you
would, to wrestle with this; when you are addressing God,
or when the subject of God comes up in conversation, what
happens in your mind? What do you think about?

M.M. I can answer that because it is something that I think about
a great deal. I may not answer it as definitely as many
might hope, but I will answer it as truthfully as possible.
How do I arrive first of all at the notion of God? For me
the notion of God comes primarily from a sense, probably the deepest spiritual experience that I have ever had,
of the oneness of life. Everything, I am profoundly convinced, is connected with everything else; the universe,
my life, the past, the future, all this is a oneness, in which
each part bears a relation to each other part. Now, it is
inconceivable to me that there could be this oneness without a One: a unitary spirit behind it. I see in the world,
the phenomenal world, in nature which I love very much,
in the achievements of men which I admire very much, in
myself, in my responses and reactions to the world, I see
this mysterious connection, this oneness, which to me
presupposes one being, a oneness behind all life. Nothing
that could happen in exploring the universe, or finding out
about life, affects that idea; on the contrary, each new
discovery embellishes, enlarges, it. There is no conflict at
all. I have also noticed that the greatest scientists, men
like Einstein, are more than anyone else aware of this,
because they see scientifically what we see intuitively
—this fact that there is nothing which you can explore
in the universe which is not related to everything else.
As Blake indicates majestically, if we could understand
perfectly a grain of sand we should understand the uni-

verse. That, to me, says God. Now then, how do I see this God? If it were not for the Christian religion, I should see no more of God than that. I should content myself with saying that there is a oneness, a spirit animating this universe.

R.T. You have talked about a God who unified, but this could be just an impersonal force.

M.M. The next step is one of faith, but one which, I contend, is borne out by the very shape and colour and flavour of the universe, as well as by everything that has been experienced about it. That spirit is a loving spirit, not a hating spirit, or an indifferent spirit; a creative, not a destructive, spirit. We recognise its hand in all the creativity of men, and we recognise its opposite in all the destructiveness of men; we recognise its hand in art, because art is an image of this unity of the universe. So we now arrive at the point that there is a spirit, and this spirit is a spirit of love, not of hate or indifference, a spirit of creativity, not of destructiveness. If it were not for the Gospels, there I should stop, and I shouldn't mind stopping there. Christianity is not something I needed in this sense, because I could perfectly comfortably and happily live and die on the basis of what I have just said.

R.T. How, before the Gospels, or in spite of the Gospels, or instead of the Gospels, did you come to the conclusion that this spirit was loving? On what evidence?

M.M. On the evidence first of all of the actual world itself. I mean its colours, its scents, its seasons, all the things that I find enchanting; these are, to me, an expression of love. Then again, not always, but in one's highest moments, so are one's closest and truest human relationships. If you are capable, if a man is capable of this emotion of love, which we all recognise, as every civilisation has recognised, and as even savages recognise, as the highest impulse which we can feel about another human being, to the point that we prefer another human being's interests to our own, this suggests to me at once—more than suggests, involves the assumption—that the spirit which has

created us partakes of the nature of this love because it
could only partake of the highest, not the lowest. I once
read in a book by some Flemish mystic that hunger presupposes the existence of bread; similarly, I think that this
longing that all men have had since the beginning of time,
and in all circumstances, and will always have until the end
of time, whatever may happen—that this longing presupposes the existence of what is longed for. But as I say,
if it were not for the Christian Gospels, there the matter
would rest, and there it would rest perfectly happily and
contentedly so far as I am concerned.

R.T. Malcolm, have you had what could be described as a
present-day mystical experience of Jesus Christ?

M.M. I can't say 'no' to that, although I wish to explain that I
am by temperament an extremely sceptical person. I don't
believe in a lot that people say about their religious experiences. I'm very sceptical about the fantasies of mysticism
altogether. I don't believe in visions myself, since I have
never had one, but on the other hand, as I have continued
to think about the Christian religion, begun to read the
Gospels and related literature, particularly contemporary
writings, I have had a sense of the presence of Christ. Perhaps the particular moment was when I was making some
films in the Holy Land for television; on the road to
Emmaus I understood, in a particularly vivid and personal
way, that there is someone else, a third man, who will
join one and help one along the way. On his own, no
human being can hope to overcome the wickedness and
selfishness inherent in his nature. It's absolutely impossible.
Yet Christians have been able to do this because there is
this help available. I know that this help *is* available; I
know I can call on it myself. To realise this is a very
different thing from a Damascus Road experience, or the
kind of visions and voices that have been seen and heard.
The person who put it best for me was the writer whose
work, to me, is the most perfect expression of Christianity in our time—though she herself was not a Christian in

any formal sense. I mean Simone Weil. Describing a moment of illumination she says that Christ came down and took possession of her. I can understand that, because there is a point when the captivation of Christ, and of his teaching, is so great that it is exactly like being obsessed with someone else. One is, as Simone Weil puts it, in the most literal sense possessed.

R.T. That is an interesting phrase—that Christ came down and captivated her. Do you believe that Christians are those people whom he has captivated, or those who have sought his captivation?

M.M. I would not be dogmatic about that, because I am absolutely convinced that there are many routes to Christ and his mercies. I think that all any man can do is to try to find his own way, and, if he is capable of communicating, perhaps to tell others about his adventures, so that he may conceivably help them. But I think there are an infinite number of ways, from the absolutely simple illumination that we associate with the saints, past and present, to the agonising struggle of someone like Kierkegaard to attain the sort of understanding of Christ and relationship with him that he longed for.

R.T. What triggers it off in a man, though? This is a wild generalisation, but I think of the masses and masses of people who never give a thought to God or Jesus Christ or eternity, and then of the others that do. I know I am hovering here on a Calvinistic notion, but is it God who chooses a few, or is this something that can happen for all of us? What I am wondering about here is what starts it in a man, what awakens a man to the possibility that life is more than what he just sees on this earth?

M.M. We don't know. We say that there are millions of people who never think of God, but we don't know; we can never really know. It appears like that, but we can never tell. One gets some very strange surprises. I firmly believe that there is a divine light in every human being ever born or to be born. I don't think any life can be lived in total darkness, but of course I agree with you that the actual gift of experiencing the light consciously, and still more of being able to convey the nature of that light, is a somewhat rare thing. This is part of the general mystery of our being, but I am absolutely sure that when we do understand we shall see that, first of all, the illumination was much more widespread than appears to us to be the case, and, secondly, that it was necessary for this light to shine through certain individuals whose particular role this has just happened to be. I have never myself met a soul in total darkness, except for those who are mad. Unfortunately, when people are mad—and our civilisation is ever producing more who are mad—then you have a feeling of their being in total darkness. Even with them, though, you never know. My eldest son, a dedicated Christian if ever there was one, worked for a while as a helper in an institution which cares for the incurably mentally sick. I asked him whether he was ever afraid, especially when dealing with homicidal cases. No, he said; they too, were God's children. What could he do for them? I asked. He told me that he read the New Testament to them in the hope that a phrase, or even a word, some little glimmer of its light, might reach them. Surely, God would not let so sweet a hope quite fail.

On that same visit to the Holy Land I came to feel quite certain that not even Judas had irretrievably cut himself off from the love of God.

R.T. We come now to the Gospels and the incredible event of Jesus Christ.

M.M. Yes. The Gospels as I have grown to understand them and this is a later thing . . .

R.T. How late exactly?

M.M. I should have said that it was only in the last ten year that I have come to understand how, through the Gospels we can see God in the shape of a man, and a man in the shape of God, thereby grasping what I think is the most wonderful concept of all of God as a father and of the human race as a family; not equal as political idealists like to pretend, not at all, but equal as brothers and sisters in a family are equal. Some are clever, some are stupid, some are attractive, some are boring, some are ugly, some are beautiful; all this is true, but the moment that you have a sense of a family and a father these differences become insignificant, as they do in a family, and all are equal. No one in a family would say that a plain sister is inferior to a pretty one; not inside a family, only outside. If this Christian notion is correct, and I am profoundly convinced that it is, then it answers the question of the relationship between man and man. From the Christian Gospels, and their presentation of Christ's captivating personality, then, I have been able to fathom the mysterious circumstances that he was God, and that in him God became man. These are assumptions that I find no difficulty over at all. They are not even particularly miraculous; certainly no more so than much else that we take for granted about the material universe. There is, in any case, a massive weight of evidence in support of them which one can read in the lives of people who have accepted their validity, and been transformed thereby.

R.T. What do you mean when you say that this man was God?

M.M. I mean that through the character of this man and the teaching of this man I may understand God, and I may understand what God wants for and from man.

R.T. What is it about Jesus Christ that convinces you of this difference in him?

M.M. The Jesus who emerges from the Gospels is this man who tells me, who explains to me, the ways of God, and, I also think, who explains to God the ways of man. In other words, he is an intermediary between God and men who reveals in his person and in his life the unity that we have sensed, and who translates it into individual terms.

R.T. What individual acts or attitudes of his show this?

M.M. Primarily, of course, his death. That is the essential thing; if that hadn't happened, then he would only have been one more wonderful teacher; but his death and all that fol-

lowed from it seems to me clearly to establish the relationship between God and his creation.

R.T. Talk to me about his death. What do you think was
going on at Calvary?

M.M. I think that men had to be shown that the way to revelation was through suffering; not, as they may have been
inclined to think, that the way was through happiness. A
great image revelatory of this was absolutely essential.
They had also to be shown that what they must worship is,
in earthly terms, defeat, not, as they thought, victory;
that they must worship what in earthly terms is weak, not
what has hitherto been thought of as strength; that this
image of a man dying because of the truth that he embodied, established for ever what truth is—something you
die for.

R.T. The cross was a great counterblast, then, against the
view that this world is complete in itself or an end in
itself?

M.M. That is why, coinciding as it did with that fantastic
Roman Empire, and stating the exact opposite proposition
to what that empire was built on—that is why it swept
through men's hearts, why it had this incredible effect on
them, as it still does because it is a great illumination.
You see it's a natural impulse in man, the jungle man, to
think that he must attach himself to power, because that
would defend him; that he must accumulate wealth, because that will win him respect; that he must make men
afraid of him, because then they will do what he wants.
Now the exact opposite proposition had to be established,
and Christ established it—that the exact opposite of the
jungle man's assumption was the truth.

R.T. And this is how you understand the Atonement?

M.M. Absolutely. Absolutely.

R.T. You are quite sure there was a Resurrection?

M.M. I am sure there was a Resurrection, but I don't in the least
care whether the stone was moved or not moved, or what
anybody saw, or anything like that. I am absolutely indifferent to that. But there must have been a Resurrection

because Christ is alive now. Christ is alive now, two thousand years later. There is no question at all about that.

R.T. What do you mean when you say that he is alive now?

M.M. He is alive now in the sense that he exists now as a person who can be reached.

R.T. You believe you can have a personal reationship with Jesus Christ now?

M.M. I believe that Jesus Christ is alive now, that, as it were, his life is still valid, so that it is possible, not only to hear and learn, but *experience,* the truths that he propounded. Now you may say that this is not quite what Christians mean, and I daresay it isn't, but I really can't help that. I know absolutely, without any question, that you can derive strength and illumination from a relationship with the man in the Gospels which you cannot achieve, we'll say for instance with Socrates, who was a very wise and good man who also died.

R.T. There is a sense that Jesus is alive now, in a way that Socrates is not alive now?

M.M. Socrates is not alive now, although I can read Socrates and know his thoughts, which are very elevating thoughts, and read about his death, which was a very noble death.

R.T. But there is the very mysterious presence of Jesus Christ now?

M.M. Yes, and that is the Resurrection; that is what I, at any rate, mean by the living Christ. In some unique way the thought and teaching and persona of this man are still here, although there are plenty of people from whom, in an earthly sense, one might learn more because they are more sophisticated and complicated. With Jesus there is some unique quality which has inspired our civilisation. If this inspiration ever dried up, then our civilisation would be over.

R.T. Does the element of the miraculous in the Gospels worry you at all?

M.M. Not at all. I don't find the miracles in any way puzzling. Christ used to say to the people he miraculously cured that their sins were forgiven them; in other words, he relieved them of their guilt. If you relieve people of their guilt, you also relieve them of their sickness, because physical imperfections are only a manifestation of spiritual imperfection. I find the miracles much more realistic than much modern medicine, and than all modern psychiatry. I think that Christ was a great healer because he was a man of infinite wisdom who understood exactly what life was about in a way that nobody else ever has. His method of dealing with the sick and infirm was a completely comprehensible one. He understood that what is the matter with men, whether mentally, physically or spiritually, is their fear and guilt, and that if you deliver them from fear and guilt they become well. Now you may say that this couldn't apply to every sick person, and it's quite possible it couldn't; but it certainly applied to the people Christ cured and made whole. For instance, a lot of the sick that he dealt with were off their heads, mad, and he described them as being possessed by evil spirits. And many today, in the light of their own experience of dealing with the mentally afflicted, know that madness *is* possession by an evil spirit. If you can exorcise that evil spirit, and drive it away by introducing the opposite principle—which is the principle of love and harmony rather than of violence and disharmony—a cure automatically follows.

R.T. Is evil personal, as good is personal in God?

M.M. Oh, I think so. There is a devil—a spirit of evil in us tugging at us to make us animals rather than angels.

R.T. Couldn't this just be the fact that evolutionarily we are still very much nearer the jungle?

M.M. It could be, yes. But even if that was so it wouldn't alter the situation. That situation may have arisen as a result of an evolutionary process, but it's still the same situation.

R.T. But it would cancel out the need to have a personal devil.

M.M. I am not particular about a personal devil. I shan't be distressed if there isn't one, but I am absolutely sure that there is a great spirit or force of evil to which men can succumb, individually and collectively, and that this force makes them animals rather than spiritual beings, makes them kill and destroy rather than love and create.

R.T. Do you think that Jesus was a product of evolution, or do you think that this was a miraculous intervention?

M.M. I am always allergic to miraculous interventions because I don't observe them in life, and I don't think that it makes Jesus any more remarkable if he represents a miraculous intervention than if a process which began when we were created found its culmination in him. It's again a matter of no great moment as far as I am concerned. The thing that matters to me is that he lived and lives.

R.T. So the Virgin Birth doesn't really figure?

M.M. Not in the least. It's understandable, of course, that people were awed, and rightly awed, by this man; by the influence he exerted, and by the stupendous effect of his words and thoughts, transforming the world's darkness into light. So, naturally, they thought he couldn't have come into the world as we did. I can't see that it's of any importance really; it's a natural thought, but how Christ came into the world doesn't matter.

R.T. It matters to me, Malcolm, in this sense, that if Jesus is, shall we say, the apex of an evolutionary process, why has there only ever been one of him, or one of his quality? I know myself well enough to realise that even if I lived to be a hundred, I shall still want to get down on my knees and say 'Lord' to him, and yet two thousand years have passed, and we haven't another Jesus Christ.

M.M. Rather than seeing him as the apex of an evolutionary process, I prefer to regard him as a consequence of the creation of life. We don't know how life began, or when it began. But creation presupposes a Creator whom we call God. As a part of some divine purpose Jesus was born, Jesus lived, Jesus taught, Jesus died. If you call that the apex of an evolutionary process, you demean it in actual fact. Nor would it follow at all. Evolution has at best proved to be a very rough-and-ready sketchy kind of a half-guess at something. I don't think it amounts to more than that, though, as usual, much too much importance has been attributed to it. For instance, man has deduced from the theory of evolution such absurdities as the survival of the fittest, which is patently ridiculous. Likewise, the whole system of evolutionary economics which is now a completely exploded myth.

R.T.   Evolution in morals?

M.M.   Certainly, in morals—probably the most ludicrous deduction of all.

R.T.   But hasn't the same thing been done with Christianity?

M.M.   Curiously enough, no, doubtless because the essential truth of Christianity is so strong. There are a certain number of legends associated with Christianity certainly, of a fairly harmless nature, but in modern times no one has been forced to believe in them, or been thought any the worse of for not believing in them. In my opinion these legends are much less harmful than scientific fallacies because they have no implications. If you say to me that St Bernadette saw a vision of the Virgin Mary in the grotto at Lourdes, I might agree or not agree, but it's a perfectly harmless thing, anyway. If you say to me that men are so made that the strongest kicks the weakest in the teeth and then the strongest survive, and go on to argue that if you apply this to economics you will get a happy society, you have done an irreparable wrong as we know, as we have seen. I think the legend is far less harmful than the fallacy; by comparison it's relatively charming.

R.T.   You said that your religious position arose out of asking the question: 'What is it all about?' When I asked Marghanita Laski about this she said: 'There is no possible answer to that, so I do not tease my brain asking the question.' Do you feel that it is possible for us ever to come to any kind of answer that can be satisfactory?

M.M.   Yes. I think Christ provides an answer, which I find completely satisfying.

R.T.   What is that?

M.M.   That we live to the extent that we die. That the purpose of life is to love God and love our neighbour. That in so far as we achieve this we establish a relationship with our Creator, with the essential purpose of being here, and with the extraordinary individual, Jesus Christ, who came into the world and explained this.

R.T. What is the guarantee that what you think you are finding is valid, is right?

M.M. In a word—faith, in which I profoundly believe. In this I have with me all the wise men of our civilisation who ever lived. I do not think that the intellect, reason, can produce an answer to life, and I don't know of any person for whom I have any respect, including many scientists, among them the greatest, who has not seen that reason is an inadequate instrument, and that one can only appreciate what life is about through this other dimension which we call faith.

R.T. How is this corroborated? Or does it need to be corroborated?

M.M. It is self-corroborating, because we know it, and if we don't know it we haven't got faith.

R.T. You mean this is an absolute knowledge?

M.M. To me, yes. It is of course supported by the fact that there are all these others who had this faith, and that it would be rather extraordinary if each one of them was simply a self-deluded fool, considering that such people are by universal consent the most creative minds and spirits of our civilisation. That in itself is not a proof. There is also the fact that people one has known who strike one as good and true are people who in some degree or another have this faith. The inadequacy of the mind alone is something that is absolutely and dramatically illustrated at every point; everything is built on faith, and faith is the essence of everything.

R.T. But Malcolm, it was asking a tremendous lot when Jesus said to the young rich ruler, 'Sell all you have and follow me.' The demand was total. Aren't people entitled to some kind of assurance that what they are doing is either sane or sensible or reasonable or right?

M.M. Yes, they are entitled to that assurance. The assurance is provided, because to the degree that they have this faith they know it's true. In other words, as Pascal says: 'Whoever looks for God has found him.' Faith contains its own justification. There is also a mountain of confirmatory evidence in the innumerable cases of all sorts and conditions of people, from the most simple and unsophisticated to the most complicated intelligences that have ever been, who have all reached the same conclusion and found the same certainty. No man that I know of has been able to live a whole life without faith, on a basis of the intellect solely. I doubt if there has ever been a single case of it.

R.T. When you say *this* faith, what is this faith, what is it faith in?

M.M. In my particular case, it is in and about the Christian religion.

R.T. Let us talk about what it is for you.

M.M. For me it is the Christian religion, as contained in the Gospels.

R.T. What is contained?

M.M. The message that Christ came to tell us—that we are children of God, and as children of God we are brothers and sisters in one human family; that this human family has a destiny which is beyond the world of time and space and mortality, but which is yet realisable through the experience of living in the world; and that if we live according to the terms that Christ proposed we may know and participate in this destiny. Such was Christ's message, enunciated after him so clearly by the Apostles, and subsequently elaborated and fulfilled through the tradition of the Christian religion at its best—a tradition which, with innumerable lapses into wickedness and abysmal horror, has somehow been carried on. In other words, through the illumination that Christ provided in his life, we can become new men and find a new happiness and a new zest and a new understanding. That's the Christian religion in brief to me. I read about it and continue to think about it, and note its presentation from generation to generation. In our time, for me it has been presented by people like

Simone Weil and Bonhoeffer and Kierkegaard—new presentations of the same everlasting gospel.

It's quite conceivable, in my opinion, that within the next decades what is called Western civilisation may finally expire, as other civilisations have before it, and that institutional Christianity will be extinguished with it. If this were so, and it may well be so, it wouldn't alter my feeling in the slightest degree. I know that Christianity is true, I believe it. I would venture to put my own interpretation on some of its aspects, but essentially it's true. I propose through my remaining years to attempt to live by it and for it. In so far as I am able to communicate with my fellows, it is what I will communicate to them; this little light, if I am spared the strength to keep it going, will continue to shine.

R.T. I want to talk now about death. I imagine, Malcolm, that you have had to face this in your personal experience. What do you think about dying? What do you think happens to people when they die? There are all kinds of theories in Christian theology—you go to sleep and you wake up at the Last Judgment, or the Nonconformist view, sudden death, sudden glory. Here we are with somebody that we love and they die. Now the human mind wants to make sense of this. I have been in the position many, many times as a clergyman of ministering to people who want to know if the dead person whom they loved is alive. Is he all right, will they see him, will they be together again? These are very simple questions, but very, very important human questions, and I think the Church, or maybe the Christian faith itself, has been so nebulous here that the hungry sheep have looked up and haven't been fed.

M.M. Of course, this is one of the fundamental things. Death is essentially the reason for religion. We could probably rub along if it wasn't for death, but we can't because of the fact of death. First of all, my own feeling about it is this—that it is impossible to know. There are certain things we can never know, and the exact circumstances of dying, and what happens afterwards, are among them. Secondly, I have an absolute conviction, without any qualification whatsoever, that this life that we live in time and space for threescore years and ten is not the whole story; that it is only part of a larger story. Therefore, death cannot be for others, or for one's self, an end, any more than birth is a beginning. Death is part of a larger pattern; it fits into a larger, eternal scale, not simply a time scale. This is something I know. Whether the ego, or what we call the personality, remains intact, or remains at all, whether the separate individuality as we know it remains, are questions to which I don't know the answers. No one knows, and no one ever will know. I think of my own death as something which will transform my way of living into another mode of living rather than as an end; and one thinks of others whom one has loved and who have died as equally participating in that other existence, in that larger dimension. To me this is completely satisfying. I don't want to know any more than this. I'm perfectly content with it. I can honestly say that I have never been afraid of death, and I am less afraid of it now than ever. I just look forward to it as something that will happen. I should like to be spared, obviously, from mental collapse, because I should hate to be that kind of burden on people, but even so I am perfectly certain that if one were so afflicted, it would somehow be part of this larger plan, and as such must be acceptable. I think the most important sentence in the whole Christian religion, devotionally speaking, is 'Thy will be done.' This is the essential sentence to be able to say, especially in relation to death.

R.T. Have you any kind of a glimpse, though, into a kind of life that doesn't include self-consciousness or awareness? When I hear people say, as you have said, that after death we get caught up in some new dimension, to me the whole glory of human beings is that we are each a different being, and I am only just beginning to explore the wonder and the mystery of human relationship, of me being related to you, another human being, and it seems to me a little glib when people say, well, I could well do without this, or I wouldn't mind if this was all lost. It seems to me that we are cutting something out here that is very important.

M.M. What I said was that to me it's obvious that this existence in a body, in time, on the earth, in this tiny corner of the universe, is part of a larger existence, and that one's relationship to that larger existence will be manifest when one dies here. I think that you are making the mistake of applying a false yardstick. You say that we can only comprehend life in terms of our own egos, and of course that is so, because you are so living at this moment, but if you imagine yourself not living in that way, then some other mode of existence becomes equally comprehensible.

R.T. But I can't imagine myself living in any other way than being myself, or being me.

M.M. Clearly, but that doesn't mean that you won't live in another way: it only means that you can't imagine it.

R.T. But in the New Testament it states that Jesus rose from the dead, and he was the same Jesus that the disciples had known before he died, and he said 'God is not the God of the dead but of the living, he is the God of Abraham and Isaac.' There seems to be implied in the New Testament some kind of self-continuity. Life after death will obviously be more self-less, it obviously will not be egocentric, but it seems to me that there is a question here that has to be faced.

M.M. I don't see it that way. Obviously, the disciples when they saw Christ, could only see him as they knew him, because they had no other shape in which they could possibly see him, but that doesn't mean that after his death and his Resurrection he was the same person. It only means that they saw him in that way. If Shakespeare kills off one of his characters, and then brings him in as a ghost, it is just as he was in life. This is the only way he can connect the ghost on the stage with the man who was killed.

I think that if you can accept the incredible notion of being here for so short a while, and not knowing how you got here, you ought to be able to accept the mystery of life after death. We are like one of these insects that fly round a lamp, and inside twenty-four hours they have come and gone—this is our earthly life. We haven't the faintest notion what we are at, where we come from, where we are going, if anywhere. We live on a tiny corner of a vast universe which—I am no use at these things—stretches for thousands and thousands of light-years, etc. If we can accept that, we can accept anything, and we have to accept that, because that is in fact our situation.

What it all boils down to is: Do we believe that the significance of our being is exhausted by *this* experience of living? I say it cannot be. I am convinced that the evidence against this is overwhelming. Plenty of people have said that I say this because I have a big ego. I don't think it is only that; but even if it were, all right then we have been born into this world as little tiny creatures with big egos, and the fact that we have big egos must in itself have some significance. But if these people we love were gone for ever we wouldn't wish to love them any less, we wouldn't part from them in any different way, we wouldn't think of them any differently. I believe that we must trust in God, which I do. I believe that in being here, we are fulfilling some purpose of his; whatever that purpose is it is the best purpose that we can have. If that purpose involves meeting again after death as we have known one another here, then we *shall* meet again: if it is not God's purpose, then we shan't. In eternity we shall have no worries about it. I think that is all there is really to say about it. I have seen people dead in war. I think it's a dreadful thing that we in our wickedness should kill those who are young, those whose lives are not fulfilled, but the actual fact of death is not a terrifying thing at all.

R.T. What experiences give you now the deepest joy—I'm not talking about happiness, but joy?

M.M. I can answer that very easily. For me the only great joy is understanding. This means being attuned to God, to the moral purpose of the universe, to the destiny of the human race that I belong to, to the things that are good—this is joy, and it is of course an experience. I find it sometimes in, for instance, music; now that I am older I find that music is the most appealing of the arts. I usen't to, but now I do.

R.T. I'm so pleased to hear that, because music hasn't happened to me yet.

M.M. Well it will. You will find that, because music is so detached from everything else, through it you touch God. That's joy. Misery is to be shut off and in darkness, and of course, alas, there is still no way of avoiding that. Suddenly it's gone; the light of awareness, gone; as you might suddenly lose your love for a person. It's gone, blotted out, and you are in darkness, confined in that terrible little dungeon of the ego, that little dark dungeon down there, tortured by fears, appetites, frustrations, ambitions, greed—all these things crowd in on you like invisible devils, and there you are—lost. That's hell. People ask what hell is. I say that is hell, and that's what it's going to be like. Then suddenly, equally unaccountably, through maybe a sight of nature, or of a loved face, or maybe a snatch of music, or just through thinking, being perceptive, it comes back—snap—almost like that—you are in tune, you are in communion; you are back in relationship with God and the moral nature of the universe, and everything is clear; there is nothing to be afraid of, and there is only joy, and only love; it's quite extraordinary.

R.T. So we reach a stage where God is personal, where Jesus is personal, where Jesus is alive and you are in relationship with God and with Jesus Christ. Now what form does your communion with God and Jesus Christ take? In other words how do you understand praying?

M.M. I should have had great difficulty in answering that at one time. I take the view that everybody prays. There is nobody who doesn't pray, and there is nobody who doesn't spare some little moment in his life to look outside his ego. But of late I have learnt more about this. Let's be perfectly factual. I wake up in the morning, and I like to begin the day by thinking what life is about, rather than plunging into the sort of things one is going to have to do. So I like to read the Gospels, the Epistles, St Augustine, the metaphysical poets like George Herbert, whom I consider to be the most exquisite religious poet in the English language. I read a bit, and then my mind dwells on what I've read, and this I consider to be prayer. Yes, that is prayer. It doesn't for some reason appeal to me to make any specific requests about my personal affairs because I do not consider they are likely to be of any great interest, but I don't criticise those who do.

R.T. But what about this struggle with sin, with worldliness? You said earlier that we need the help that God can give us. Are you never conscious that you need to turn to God and say 'Look I am in a hopeless condition, incapable and powerless?'

M.M. My impulse, when the darkness sweeps me up, is not to say: 'Please let me out of the darkness,' but to seek the light which I know is there. I am frightened like a child in a dark room; I look for the window, and Christ is the window. That's the thing; he is a window, and when you look, out there is a wonderful vista. What's the darkness now?

R.T. Malcolm, do you ever address God?

M.M. Yes I do sometimes, but not in the sense of requests. I wrote a little prayer recently and I'll read it to you—

'O God, stay with me; let no word cross my lips that is not Your word, no thoughts enter my mind that are not Your thoughts, no deed ever be done or entertained by me that is not Your deed, Amen.'

That was my own prayer, and its form is an exception. That is why I wrote it down, because I don't very often feel induced to address my Creator in that sort of way. To me prayer is a sort of understanding . . .

R.T. What I am after here, Malcolm, is that St Paul said: 'In him I live and move and have my being;' other people say: 'I enjoy God.' What I want to know from you is this—Do you believe that God is addressable?

M.M. Oh, certainly.

R.T. Can you address God in a way that is different from addressing nature?

M.M. My little prayer is addressed to God, but it so happens that it's not my own practice to make this kind of personal address, but of course I believe in God as personal. Otherwise prayer wouldn't work; it wouldn't have any meaning.

R.T. God has sufficiently objective reality, that although you don't know his form, his nature, and so on, God is such that you can say 'O God'?

M.M. Most certainly. God is the father, we are a family.

R.T. Malcolm, you know something of the mystics, and one of the things they talk about which fascinates me, fascinates me with horror almost, is what they describe as 'the dark night of the soul'. Not that I have suffered in this way, but I know what it is like to be in the darkness which you described earlier. I have known what it is like to go for months with no sense of God. God has gone; religion is an illusion; I have been a fool for believing it; this life is all there is; it's all crazy and mad. This is terribly deep, and fills me with despair. Then the light breaks through again, but the mystics seem to be saying, yes, these are simple forms of this kind of spiritual suffering, but the time will come when, in order to be fashioned as God wants you to be fashioned, you must go through 'the dark night of the soul,' and I must say that if it's infinitely worse than what I have already experienced this frightens me.

M.M. First of all I'm sure it's not, because I am sure that what you have described, and what we all recognise, is 'the dark night of the soul'. As I understand it from St John of the Cross, and he went most deeply into this, it is something that comes always shortly before a moment of illumination, so that I don't think you have any occasion to fear. Of course it's the only thing to fear; there is nothing else to fear at all, nothing at all. Nobody can hurt us, nobody can rob us, not in any real way; but we can be shut off, alas, from the love of God, and if we are, better not to have been born.

R.T.   I'm going to be a little bit complicated now. When I go
        through a time now when God seems to have gone,
        because I have a lot of experience from the past when it
        has been like that, but he has come back again, so I can
        face, shall I say, these wilderness experiences now, and
        hold on to my faith, and say that all I have to do is to
        hold on because the darkness will pass. Now I sometimes
        wonder if the 'dark night of the soul' is the time when
        that consolation is taken from you, so that you are left
        without hope altogether?

M.M.   But surely that is where Christ comes in. He's always
        standing by; his help is always available.

R.T.   You don't think there is a specific dark night of the soul?
        You think there are many dark nights?

M.M.   Yes, and if there was a specific one it would only be an
        intensification of what has already been experienced.
        Because of Christ there can never be a dark night that
        doesn't end. The darkness always comes to an end because
        Christ is here with us now. If he weren't, then when this
        darkness came down we might never emerge from it.

R.T.   You have said that you use the Bible in your prayer times.
        Why is it that the Bible for most people—again a wild
        generalisation—is a boring book that is just never read?

M.M.   Partly because many people unfortunately are illiterate.
        Our education system is making everyone more and more
        illiterate. Once people knew the Bible and loved the Bible
        as children; not just as Christians, but because it is one of
        the greatest works of literature which exist. If the Christian
        religion and everything connected with it disappeared,
        the Authorised Version of the Bible would still be among
        the three or four supremely great books in the English
        language. That is absolutely certain. Unfortunately, I sup-
        pose it's the way it's presented to people, the way it's read
        to them, particularly in these new translations. Nowadays
        when I go to church I have to take an Authorised Version
        with me in order not to listen to the dreadful gibberish
        that's liable to be read out to me. It may seem like a

paradox, but, in my opinion, looking for the Bible's meaning has destroyed the Bible. The Bible is more than meaning, and if you take a passage and look only for its meaning you lose so much. If poetry were to be approached in a similar way everybody would say it was a very philistine thing to do.

R.T. But meaning is important.

M.M. Yes, meaning is important; and the meaning is there, capable of being grasped. But the moment you make the meaning identical with the words, and get some tenth-rate writer to extract the meaning and put it down, you are making, I think, a great mistake, and taking away from people the joy of the Bible. You know here we needn't be talking about religion at all. With people of little or no education beautiful cadences came into their speech because they knew this one great book, the Authorised Version of the Bible. Think of Bunyan, a writer of supreme and unique genius who knew no other book. The Bible is considered to be something which is out-of-date. It is a most extraordinary idea. I heard a man on the radio complaining that the God of Westminster Abbey is a mediaeval God. But God can't be mediaeval, or modern, or ancient; he's eternal or nothing. It's as though people of the Middle Ages had complained that the God of the New Testament is a Judaic God, and therefore they were not interested in him. They wanted a mediaeval God. This notion of the out-of-dateness of the Bible is utterly absurd, but is implanted in people's minds, I regret to say, to a great extent by the clergy. People say that the Bible is a boring book, that it belongs to the past, but they don't say that about Shakespeare because the people who teach Shakespeare are zealous for Shakespeare.

R.T. It doesn't worry you when people say that our selves, our self-consciousness, who we are, everything we are, is all a manifestation of that piece of matter which exists in our head that we call a brain, and when the brain disintegrates that is the total disintegration of us?

M.M. It doesn't worry me at all, because if that turns out to be true I shall not be in a position to realise that I had been wrong, but I think that every single thing I know or have observed suggests the contrary—that I am more than my nervous system, and on that supposition I live. If it could be shown that I have been making a mistake, even then, if it were possible to form a judgment on it, I should prefer to have lived on a basis of this mistake. I shall never be in a position to reach a conclusion about this, but even if you could prove to me to your satisfaction, that what you say might be true, is true, I would still think it better to live on the assumption that it wasn't, with a strong feeling that I should be correct in doing that.

R.T. You are not at all bothered by these people who say that we are just animated lumps of matter?

M.M. I'm not, because I am quite sure that animated lumps of matter don't write the plays of Shakespeare; they don't discover the Theory of Relativity, and since man has done this it is evidently untrue that we are only animated lumps of matter.

R.T. How do you reconcile your belief in the loving purposes of God with the birth of Mongol children and mentally defective children. We have just heard that Helen Keller has died who was born deaf, dumb and blind. Do you think that these tragedies are due to the stupidity of man at some point?

M.M. Not at all. I think it is part of the pattern of life. What's more I think it's an essential part. Imagine human life being drained of suffering! If you could find some means of doing that, you would not ennoble it; you would demean it. Everything I have learnt, whatever it might be —very little I fear—has been learnt through suffering.

R.T. Would you be willing to tell me in what way, or is that too personal?

M.M. Not at all. I learned not to lose my temper through the grief and contrition which afflicted me when I became violently angry with someone infinitely dear to me who had gone temporarily mad. I lost my temper, which is a very easy thing to do, and I marvel, incidentally, that people who look after the mentally sick are able to restrain themselves as they do.

R.T. You mean the fact that this person was mentally ill made you angry with the person.

M.M. Yes, because I hate the unreason, the animality, the almost bestiality of people when they are mad. I lost my temper, and then I realised that this was an utterly evil thing to do, that it was a thing which damaged me, that it could only add to the pain and anguish of someone I loved sorely pressed by a terrible misfortune. I decided that it must never occur again.

R.T. Did it damage the other person?

M.M. Certainly. It always does damage the other person, but of course the thing that one is conscious of is the damage it does to one's self. This was a situation in which someone was sick. If the person had been sick with a broken leg or lung trouble, one would have been ashamed to be other than solicitous, but because it was this scourge of our society, mental disturbance, it produced in me violent anger. I realised in a moment of absolute illumination which could never have come in any other way, that I had done an utterly despicable thing, and furthermore, that all anger in all circumstances is equally wicked. Of course I have been angry again, but I have never been as angry. You know there are few things one can point to in one's nature which really change, but thenceforth I was completely changed in that respect, and I could never have learnt it in any other way than through this utterly desolating experience.

Another example occurs to me. There was one point in my life when I decided to kill myself, and I swam out to sea, resolved for a variety of reasons that I didn't want to live any more. Partly it was a mood of deep depression, and partly actual difficulties. I swam out to sea until I felt myself sinking; you get a strange kind of sleepiness that afflicts you, as if you were just about to fall into a deep sleep. I thought that I would take one last look at the coast, and that would be the end. I saw the lights along the coast; and I suddenly realised that that was my home, the earth—the earth my home, and that I must stay on the earth because I belonged there until my life had run its course. Then somehow, I don't know how, I swam back. Now that was a time of great trouble for me, and it was very sad that I was forced to contemplate so contemptible an act. At the same time, it was a terrific turning point. I have never doubted since then that in all circumstances, whatever one's condition may be, or the condition of the society one lives in, or the condition of the world, life is good, and that to gain from this experience of living what has to be gained, and to learn what has to be learned, it is necessary to live out one's life to the end until the moment comes for one's release. Then, and only then, can one truly rejoice in that moment. There is no catastrophe, as it seems to me, that can befall human beings which is not an illumination, and no illumination which is not in some sense a catastrophe. It's in an age like ours, an age of great superficiality of thought, that people ask how, if God makes a Mongol, he can be a loving God. It's a very superficial thought, because a Mongol child is part of the process whereby man exists, and we can't judge how that comes about, or what are its full consequences. All we can say is that it's part of the experience of living, and, like all other parts, it can shed light or it can shed darkness. Suffering is an essential element in the Christian religion, as it is in life. After all, the cross itself is the supreme example. If Christ hadn't suffered, do you imagine that anyone would have paid the slightest attention to the religion he founded? Not at all.

R.T.   But it is a mystery that the only way in which God can make us grow up, or help us to grow up, is through suffering.

M.M.   It's a mystery in a sense, but just imagine the opposite. Supposing you eliminated suffering, what a dreadful place the world would be! I would almost rather eliminate happiness. The world would be the most ghastly place

because everything that corrects the tendency of this unspeakable little creature, man, to feel over-important and
over-pleased with himself would disappear. He's bad
enough now but he would be absolutely intolerable if he
never suffered. However, we needn't fear that.

R.T. What have you been like as a parent? I have found that
being a parent is far from easy.

M.M. Far from easy, but at the same time one of the absolutely
major things in life. I find it difficult to think of any
human circumstances which would make life intolerable,
but I think to be childless would be a truly dreadful
catastrophe. Now I've got grandchildren and I find it all
very delightful. But bringing my children up was by no
means easy, partly because of deficiencies in myself, partly
because of the war.

R.T. Give me some instances of deficiency.

M.M. Oh, well, being too egotistic.

R.T. What does that mean?

M.M. Being too concerned with my own interests. Quarrelling,
losing my temper—all the things I despise and hate which
I have done. Not sympathising with them when they failed
or when they were inadequate. Of course I married when
I was quite young, when I was twenty-four. We were
terrific wanderers, which I think was a bad thing really
in bringing up children. My wife says she has set up house
twenty-two times in the course of our marriage in all sorts
of countries.

R.T. What were your aims as a parent? Did you have any idea
how you should behave in relation to the children?

M.M. I didn't have any conscious aims. I don't have any now.
I think the only thing you can do with children is to love
them, and when they are grown up provide them with a
rest camp; somewhere they can withdraw to from the
battle and rest if they happen to be wounded or exhausted.

R.T. What about discipline?

M.M. We were poor, and poor people have to have discipline.
We had four youngish children rather near in age, and

unless you can afford to employ people to keep them in order—which we couldn't—you can't cope unless you have discipline. But it was only discipline imposed for practical reasons; it wasn't a theory. I have no theory for bringing up children at all.

R.T.   You didn't want to make them into anything?

M.M.   No, I didn't at all, except I wanted them to be good men and women, and I am happy to say they are.

R.T.   How have you found this whole business of being married? The mystery of another human being, living with another human being. I have found this one of the most demanding experiences of my life, one of the most valuable and profitable experiences and I would say that marriage is not a thing to be treated lightly or easily.

M.M.   Oh certainly not. That is why I am against making divorce any easier; very much against it, because I think that in every marriage there are plenty of occasions when you could easily bust it up. If it had been easy to bust it up I probably should have done so, and then how I should have regretted it! I have been married for over forty years, and I am more contented with my marriage now than when it started. Marriage is very difficult; it has many troubles. Sex, I think, is a frightful trouble, and I consider myself that marriage only becomes bearable when that element is largely eliminated. I think sex for procreation is a marvellous thing, and when one is young passion is a marvellous thing, but not to build on. I don't think any marriage built on sex can possibly last, because sex doesn't last and can't last, and it would be obscene if it did. If there is one thing I completely loathe in the contemporary world it is this unashamed effort to devise means to protract physical desire when in the normal way it has disappeared. Marriage, in any case, is an enormously difficult relationship, particularly if, as in our case, the individuals concerned aren't Christians. If the Christian scale of values isn't accepted then all the questions of jealousy, infidelity and so on arise and have to be fought through, and sometimes with great pain and strife.

R.T. When you said you weren't Christians, you mean at that stage you weren't consciously a Christian?

M.M. Or even unconsciously. I didn't accept the Christian view of marriage at all when I married. Marriage, in our eyes, was a purely legal arrangement.

R.T. Why did you bother to struggle through?

M.M. Well, because I loved my wife, for no other reason; and if there is one single thing I feel grateful for at this moment it would be that, more than anything else at all; far transcending anything in the way of success (utterly bogus anyway) that I might be considered to have had.

R.T. But there were times when you hated her.

M.M. I don't know that I hated, but there were times of strife, and this is a terrible thing. Marriage without the comfort of Christian morality is a stormy affair. But it can be survived.

R.T. I believe, when the storms come in my own marriage, because I believe in an eternal reference to this relationship, that it is worth working through; struggling with or being patient with the present situation, because I believe there is an end to work towards and this is part of my being a Christian.

M.M. I entirely agree with that.

R.T. What was your motivation to make your marriage work when you didn't have this eternal reference?

M.M. Without being a Christian? First of all the simple fact again of poverty, and I would here mention that I belong to a minority who think that the poor really are blessed as the New Testament tells us. There is a great blessing in poverty which is very little realised today. If you are poor, and you have children, and you accept at any rate the idea that you owe a duty to those children to bring them up, that you can't just jettison them, then to a great extent you are *committed* to a matrimonial relationship. Now I don't think this is bad, I think it is good. I approve of it, and I pity the rich who are always in the position that they have no material obstacles to shedding relationships, whether with a wife, children or anyone else. There is, of course, also the fact of love, which is a very real thing, and which endures, contrary to the modern view. I do not at all identify love and sexual desire. I think the two things coincide for a glorious period of youth, but otherwise they are separate.

R.T. What do you say to people who would like easy divorce because of people who are married before they grow up almost, before they understand. They go through the ceremony that locks them together, and yet they are completely unsuitable, and all that can accrue from such marriages will be frustration, hatred, aggressiveness. Don't you think that people ought to be allowed to break these marriages up?

M.M. Yes, I think that in the last resort they should, but if my advice was sought my advice would always be in the direction of going on trying, of saying that the difficulty is not incompatibility really but vanity, egotism, and the answer to this, as to so many things, is to escape from this prison of the ego. I would also accept the idea that in the last resort there are cases, many fewer than are commonly supposed, in which two people have definitely made a mistake; they bring out the worst in each other, and in those circumstances, with the utmost reluctance and caution, I would say it's right to break it. But they are few.

R.T. I would say, as a Christian, if only people were Christian very few marriages need to break.

M.M. I agree with that. Very, very few, surprisingly few, but I think there still would be a few. There would be people who would find it impossible to live together, because of a sort of chemistry, but they are few.

R.T. What we are doing with divorce is making it possible to go from one failure to another failure.

M.M. We are establishing a system of promiscuity, a deliberate system of promiscuity, which I think will not make for happiness at all. In fact it will make for great misery, and I try to tell that to young people, but of course they don't usually listen.

R.T. It can be said of you that it is because physical passion no longer interests you that you are condemning it. People could say, it's all very well for him, he used to enjoy these things, but now he is telling us that we mustn't. People could feel that this is a very odd position to take.

M.M. This is frequently said, and I sympathise with the thought. Some people would put it more bluntly than you politely put it. They say: Here is an old debauchee who has got sick of the senses, particularly of sex, and who therefore turns round and says it's no good. Now, I see the point, but it's not true. Nor is it true that I no longer appreciate the senses. When you are old you still appreciate the senses, as much as ever really, but in a rather different way. But I have never thought, even in the most ardent moments, that the senses could give one any ultimate satisfaction. I have always thought they were delusive, and I think so now more than ever. The reason that one tends to stress this point more now is not merely because one's old, but because society itself is so stridently insisting on the opposite proposition—including a lot of Christians and churchmen. They are all insisting that physical sex is in fact a wholly satisfactory way of achieving satisfaction. I contend with St Paul and all the Christian mystics that it's not, but that doesn't mean that in itself sex is bad, or in itself undesirable. It is undesirable as an end, not as a means. Everything that we perceive or appreciate involves the senses; this natural scene outside my window that I love so much is connected with the senses. If I couldn't smell and touch and feel, I shouldn't be able to appreciate it. But if you say to me that the significance of it is its sensual appeal, and if you go on insisting that is so, as is done with this particular aspect of sensuality which is sex, so that it becomes obsessive, then it is necessary, as it seems to me, to protest, and one protests by saying this is a delusion, a fantasy, which will not even bring the passing satisfaction promised.

R.T. You have said things earlier that have led me to believe that finally for you sex should only be used for procreation. You seem to eliminate the idea of sex as enjoyment.

M.M. Yes I do. I think that the idea of sex as enjoyment is a very dangerous one. The purpose of it is procreation, the justification of it is love; if you separate sex from procreation and love, very rapidly you turn it into a horror.

R.T. But supposing you separated it from procreation but kept enjoyment within love?

M.M. Well yes, I think that is possible, but of course the fact that you are forced, in order to do that, to cut off its procreative function, in other words to sterilise it, will tend, in my opinion, in most cases to produce quite quickly a sense of nausea. Then of course, one's attitude to this depends upon one's attitude to marriage, the family and the home. I consider that some form of marriage—and I think that monogamous marriage is probably the highest form—but some form of marriage is essential to civilisation and for bringing up children. I think the family is, and ever must be, the basic and true unit of society. If you base a relationship between two people on their achieving mutual pleasure out of it, it will very soon happen that they don't achieve mutual pleasure out of it at all. This is a fact of life which we all know, and then if they persist, using these various, to me highly disgusting, erotica of various kinds, they will very soon loathe each other, and this is what is going on in our society.

R.T. What about over-population though?

M.M. To me this is a fantasy. You see, when I was young, people used to say the poor had too many children. Or, at the time of the famine in Ireland, they would say that the Irish had too many children. We were taking the food from Ireland, and the Irish were starving, and we said they were starving because they had too many children. Now we who are sated, who have to adopt the most extravagant and ridiculous devices to consume what we produce, while watching whole vast populations getting hungrier and hungrier, overcome our feelings of guilt by persuading ourselves that these others are too numerous, have too many children. They ask for bread and we give them contraceptives! In future history books it will be said, and it will be a very ignoble entry, that just at the moment in our history when we, through our scientific and technical ingenuity, could produce virtually as much food as we wanted to, just when we were opening up and exploring the universe, we set up a great whimpering and wailing, and said there were too many people in the world. It's pitiful.

R.T. Now, Malcolm, I want to ask you about the Church. It is my strong feeling that the Church is no longer doing the job it was set up to do. The world is passing it by. People are passing it by. The life seems to have gone out of it; the relevance seems to have gone from it.

M.M. I think this is an irrefutable fact, of course. It so happens that I never really belonged to any Church, so that institutional Christianity hasn't meant very much to me. But, of course, I absolutely agree with you. If you take the Church of England, I think it's really about as moribund as it could be. If it wasn't an Established Church, many of its parish churches would just cease to exist. Similarly, Nonconformity is steadily declining, and now I think the Roman Church is beginning to run down in the same sort of way. This may be an inevitable development. It wouldn't really affect anything as far as I personally am concerned, although one must remember that whatever deficiencies the various Churches have had, it is owing to them that the Gospel remains before us; they have kept it alive. The question is: Will Christianity survive if the Churches cease to exist?

I am personally convinced that our Western European civilisation is approaching its end. This is an absolutely basic part of my thinking which governs all my feelings about the world that I live in. There is to me every symptom of our civilisation petering out. This was bound to happen sometime; it just seems to me to be happening now, when I am alive. I think there are advantages in living at a time when a civilisation is coming to an end;

in such a situation, one can much better understand the
nature of power, just as one can better understand the
nature of the body when one is sick. In a dying civilisation
one is at least not taken in by power and authority as one
easily might be when conditions are flourishing.

The Christian Church is inevitably involved in this
death of our civilisation. I can see that very clearly. If you
consider the death symptoms, the foremost is an increasing
preoccupation with the material things of life. Here the
Churches go with the popular trend, and endorse, and even
enhance, our affluent society's materialist standards. I
thought at one time that the Roman Church would be a
final bastion of the Christian religion. I imagined it as a
sort of last citadel into which, for no other reasons than
that it was the last citadel, I should probably climb myself.
But I don't think so now. It seems to be clear that the
Roman Church is going the same way as the Anglican
Church, and will expire with our expiring civilisation.

R.T. What are the marks of weakness of the institutional
Church that you discern?

M.M. In the first place, the great majority of its ministers and
clergy don't believe what they purport to believe. This is
a source of terrific weakness. Whether they are right or
wrong not to believe is neither here nor there, but the fact
is it puts them in a completely false position.

R.T. I am going to challenge you. You say the vast majority,
this is wild isn't it—the vast majority?

M.M. Yes it is wild, but I would suggest that *a* majority at any
rate don't really believe the propositions that, as beneficed
clergy, they purport to believe. In their private conversations they don't even pretend to, in my experience. If you
employed a solicitor to transfer house property, and then,
when he was having a drink with you after the deal, he
said: 'Of course I don't really believe that those clauses
mean anything,' it would seem quite disgraceful. It's the
same with a clergyman who talks lightheartedly about all
the things he's supposed to believe in and doesn't. There
is a terrific gap—a credibility gap, to use the popular ex-

pression—between what they stand up and say they believe —the Creeds they recite—and what they really believe. I can't recite these Creeds, and I never do recite them, because I don't believe them in the sense that they're set forth; but a great many clergymen don't believe them either, yet they have to say they do. Then I think the Church, like most institutions of our society, is scared, and is anxious to ingratiate itself with people, rather than to tell them the truth. Therefore it takes an extremely equivocal attitude towards many of the moral issues which arise.

R.T. Could it not be that one of the reasons why the clergy appear so unenthusiastic for the things they believe, is that it is a pretty soul-destroying job trying to convince people these days that there are any ultimate values?

M.M. It's a very difficult job, and I shouldn't blame them at all if they threw in their hand and said: 'I have had a go at this, and it just can't be done, and I am looking for another job.' I feel the utmost sympathy for them; but if you ask me why the Church is so weak—obviously an institution is weak if its ostensible aims bear little or no relation to the aims and teachings of its ministers.

R.T. What do you think the aims should be?

M.M. The Gospel, the Christian Gospel; to teach people what Christ taught; to show them how he wanted them to live, how to love God and love their fellows.

R.T. Supposing nobody came to the church where that was done?

M.M. In a way it wouldn't be surprising if nobody came, because people live in a society in which they are being induced by the most powerful method of persuasion that has ever existed on earth—I mean the mass-communication media, especially television—to believe in the exact opposite. It's perfectly understandable if a clergyman says: 'Nobody comes, and I can't go on,' but what I think is absolutely fatal is not to say that, and instead to say: 'Let's make an adjustment, and see if we can't conform what we are preaching to what these mass-communication media are recommending.' There can be no adjustment; they are opposite things. Therein lies the dilemma and fate of the Church, I am afraid.

R.T. You have said previously that you believe this civilisation is coming to an end, and you are quite sure that institutional Christianity will come to an end with it, and I agree with you; but this is contrary to what the Church has believed for two thousand years. Jesus said to Peter: 'You are the rock, and upon this rock I will build my church, and the gates of hell will not prevail against it.' Now the implication seems to be that empires can fall, kingdoms can come to an end, but the Church will always continue.

M.M. It may, of course; I'm not saying it won't, because it has survived a great many things.

R.T. But my strong feeling—and I thought you echoed this— is that for the first time the Church is not going to prevail.

M.M. I think it's very doubtful whether institutional Christianity will be able to separate itself from the general process of decomposition. But one always comes back to thinking that with God all things are possible, and it is conceivable, of course, that this whole situation might change. We can only be grateful and delighted if it does, but as of now, looking at the situation objectively, I see institutional Christianity as irretrievably a part of a world order, a civilisation, which is rushing to destruction. I don't feel particularly perturbed about it, and it doesn't alter in any way, of course, my feelings about the Christian religion. The survival of the Church to date is an extraordinary fact, and no doubt churchmen would argue that its survival indicates clearly that God had a hand in it, and wants it to survive today. It might be so but I find institutional Christianity, with certain exceptions, highly unsympathetic.

R.T. When you say that you feel civilisation is collapsing, do you think this is because the Church has failed, or do you think it is man who has refused the claims of the Church and has become world-centred—*this* world-centred—and therefore corrupt, and that this is why civilisation is collapsing?

M.M. I think both processes are taking place. It's very like the Old Testament, and I want to pay my tribute to the Old

Testament. You know people are always telling us not to bother with it, but I think it's the most extraordinary book. The whole of human history is contained in the adventures of this obscure, and in many ways maddening, people. They knew all about the decline of faith and the fall of kingdoms.

R.T. A lot of the people whom you admire and respect were men who were nurtured by the Church, and lived inside the Church. Isn't it very presumptuous of us to sit here and calmly decide that of course the Church is now coming to an end, when we owe it so much? Going back to the Old Testament—the Jews had to leave Jerusalem, the Temple was destroyed, they went into captivity in Babylon, but God kept a remnant, and in that sense the Church can never die.

M.M. I think this is absolutely true. Every Christian owes an immeasurable debt to the Church because it has kept Christ's message alive. Through its worship, through its music, through marvellous things like the Book of Common Prayer, it has enshrined the Christian religion in an artistic excellence which has enormously enhanced it. Think just of the cathedrals—the Christian cathedrals of Europe; what a contribution they have made! No one is going to pretend to himself that at the same time that this was happening there were not very corrupt men in the Church, false doctrines being preached and very wicked things being done; clearly there were. I have a pessimistic view of the future of the Church because it seems to me that many of its leaders have, of their own accord, allied themselves with the forces of this world, and that is the one disastrous thing they can do.

R.T. Shouldn't you be inside the Church being part of the pull away from the worldliness? After all, the direction of the Church has been wrong many times in the past, but, thank God, there have been people within it who have corrected it, and when I talk about the Church I mean the whole Church.

M.M. I feel deeply hostile to the general direction of the Christian Churches today, one and all, including the Roman

Catholic Church; deeply suspicious and hostile. I couldn't produce an apologia for them if I was associated with them, and I find it easier to pronounce my views, such as they are, on the Christian position, from without, rather than from within. There might be a case for being inside, but, if so, which particular denomination should be preferred? That question arises then, doesn't it? One might say the Roman Catholic Church, because Roman Catholics are more numerous, international, and altogether, in certain respects, very appealing to me, but on the other hand there are other aspects which are very unappealing. The Quakers, likewise, are very appealing, but they have certain things which are unappealing. I don't know, I have a sort of feeling at this moment that institutional Christianity is careering away in a direction that I don't approve of —you may say I should be there trying to pull it back, but I don't think that I could take that on. My own picture of the future is that our society is going in the next decades to be totally non-Christian; I mean its institutions, everything about it, will lose whatever relationship they now have with Christian religion. Then I think there will be people, in the very stressful circumstances that are likely to arise, who will still want to live as Christians, and I think they are much more likely to find themselves in the position of a Christian underground, a sort of *Maquis*. I imagine the forces of paganism occupying our world, and the Christians drawn together in those conditions, rather as I remember the surviving Christians in the U.S.S.R. who appealed to me very much as being enormously pure— simply a collection of people who, in extremely hostile circumstances, clung to their faith, and tried to cling to their Christian way of life. This might easily happen, and I hope that if I were still alive, I should be among those people.

R.T.   So much for the Church and clergymen—but what about your claim that civilisation itself is coming to an end? On what grounds do you come to this judgment?

M.M.   The basic condition for a civilisation is that there should be law and order. Obviously, this is coming to an end, the world is falling into chaos, even—perhaps especially—our Western world. Furthermore, I firmly believe that our civilisation began with the Christian religion, and has been sustained and fortified by the values of the Christian religion, by which admittedly most men have not lived, but to which they have assented, and by which the greatest of them have tried to live. The Christian religion and these values no longer prevail, they no longer mean anything at all to ordinary people. Some suppose that you can have a Christian civilisation without Christian values. I disbelieve this. I think that the basis of order is a moral order; if there is no moral order there will be no political or social order, and we see this happening. This is how civilisations end.

R.T. So we are either moving into a new kind of civilisation with a new moral order, or we are moving into a new Dark Age.

M.M. Yes, and the Dark Age is likely to intervene anyway. It is very unusual for one moral order to slide into another with no intervening chaos. There are many other symptoms. The excessive interest in eroticism is characteristic of the end of a civilisation, because it really means a growing impotence, and a fear of impotence. Then the obsessive need for excitement, vicarious excitement, which of course the games provided for the Romans, and which television provides for our population. Even the enormously complicated structure of taxation and administration is, funnily enough, a symptom of the end of a civilisation; these things become so elaborate that in the end they become insupportable because of their very elaboration. Above all, there is this truly terrible thing which afflicts materialist societies—boredom; an obsessive boredom, which I note on every hand. Mine is, admittedly, a minority view; a lot of people think that we are just on the verge of a new marvellous way of life. I see no signs of it at all myself. I notice that where our way of life is most successful materially it is most disastrous morally and spiritually; that the psychiatric wards are the largest and most crowded, and the suicides most numerous, precisely where material prosperity is greatest, where most money is spent on education.

I don't regard this at all as a gloomy point of view. If one considers the nature and present objectives of our society, I think it's much more optimistic to suppose it's going to collapse than that it's going to succeed. Its success would be a nightmare beyond all thought or belief. If a place like, for instance, California really were viable, this would be the end of everything. Consider our actual circumstances at this moment. We have made ourselves so strong that we can destroy ourselves. We spend a great part of our wealth and our research resources and so on elaborating the means to destroy ourselves and the earth. Our corner of the world is getting richer, to the point that its main preoccupation is to stimulate consumption by all sorts of asinine means; while the rest of the world is getting poorer and hungrier. And the only answer we can produce is that there are too many of the others. Our ultimate offering to our less fortunate brethren is what?— a contraceptive! I don't think any civilisation has ever produced such a contemptible product as its major offering to the world.

R.T. Do you think that there is any chance of our civilisation being redeemed?

M.M. It seems to me very unlikely, but everything is possible. All historical prognostications are false. Nobody can know, I can only say that is what it looks like to me. I sometimes think to myself: Supposing I had been the sort of person that I am, as a Roman in the time of Nero, shall we say. I should, I am sure, have said exactly what I am saying now. I should have said: The barbarians are coming in, Rome will be destroyed, our whole structure of paganism and so on is all over, nobody believes in it, the administration won't work, the expenses of adminstration exceed all bounds, the Roman Empire is top heavy and it's going to collapse. And I should have been absolutely right. The only thing I shouldn't have known was that these very obscure Christian events in a distant outpost of the empire

—events involving almost totally illiterate people, subject people, people of absolutely no interest or importance to a sophisticated, educated Roman—were going to lay the foundation of a new and an infinitely greater civilisation, that in terms of art and science and understanding was going to reach unimaginable heights.

R.T. Can you see that happening now?

M.M. I wouldn't know, and you wouldn't know. We are precisely the sort of people who above all don't and can't know.

R.T. But can you see signs of it?

M.M. I find an increasing scepticism about the utopian hopes which, in the first flush of scientific achievement, made people more or less drunk with expectation. I find that hope disappearing. I find a new mood of humility. Even these half-baked students for whom I have considerable contempt, in a blind sort of way feel dissatisfied. It's good that they should feel dissatisfied; there's nothing to be satisfied with.

R.T. If you are right and this civilisation is coming to an end, the death pangs will probably take quite a long time. In the meantime somebody has to govern, somebody has to accept responsibility, the world has to go on. Some people have to be, for instance, the managers of the Central Electricity Board or the managers of the coal mines, the fruit of whose work we enjoy. Now isn't it a little bit off to criticise people who have positions of power, depending, as we do, on somebody having it?

M.M. Of course. I entirely agree that power is necessary in a society, and it would be absurd to say that all men who exercise power are bad men, but I think you could say that all men who seek power are dangerous men, and require very careful watching. Power as a passion is a bad passion. My favourite example is in the New Testament. We read that the kingdoms of the earth are in the gift of the Devil. This is a very interesting fact which isn't sufficiently regarded. Why are they in the gift of the Devil? How can it be that the Devil has the gift of the kingdoms of the earth, and not God? The reason is that the kingdoms of the earth signify power, which is a devilish pursuit.

The other day I was turning up some old notes I had made, and I found a copy of an inscription that had been set up in the Libyan desert by a Roman centurion: 'I, serving as a captain of a legion of Rome in the Libyan desert, have learnt and pondered this thought—in life there are two pursuits, love and power, and no man can have both.' That is very much what I have in mind. The same notion arises in the Book of Genesis. Through eating the fruit of knowledge—like power, a necessary pursuit—the happiness of the Garden of Eden was destroyed.

R.T.   The Book of Genesis is a myth, but do you think the myth of the fall of man represents something true which you can observe in life now?

M.M.   I would go further and say this—that I think legends and myths are probably truer than history. As Kierkegaard says, in the case of the greatest happenings such as Christ's life and death, historicity is completely without importance. It is very important to know the history of Socrates because Socrates is dead, but the history of Christ doesn't matter because he is alive. If and when we know the final truth about human life, we shall find that the legends, or what pass for legends, are far nearer the truth than what passes for fact or science or history.

R.T.   Going back to the fall of man, one has to wrestle with this. Why is man fallen? If God is the creator and he made man good, why were the seeds of corruption in him?

M.M.   This, of course, is the most fundamental and difficult question of all. I find I can grasp it better if I think of the creation of man and the universe by God as being of the same nature as creation by man, only of course multiplied by billions and billions. On however lowly a scale, in so far as I have tried to create something in words, written or spoken, as an expression of truth, that process is painful. It's not easy or pleasurable, but it can give ecstasy. Also it contains within itself the same essential principle that, in order to reach after perfection, it has to be itself intrinsically imperfect. So I see that if God had created man perfect, man without pain, man without sin, there would have been, in this sense, no creation, any more than, if King Lear had not suffered, there would have been a play for Shakespeare to write about him. The life we know, with all its pains and ecstasies, wouldn't have existed. If you imagine your life made by a different God, made perfect, it wouldn't be life. The process of creation contains in itself its own imperfection; the pursuit of perfection is via imperfection, as the pursuit of spiritual love is via the physical body. This is how it is, and this is the majesty of it, and why it is interesting. This is why there is literature, why there is art, why there is thought, and how we may know there is a God—a loving God—whose children we all are.

A PRAYER OF ST FRANCIS

Let me conclude with a much loved prayer of St Francis of Assisi:

Lord, make me an instrument of thy peace. Where there is hatred, let me sow love; where there is injury, pardon; where there is doubt, faith; where there is despair, hope; where there is sadness, joy; where there is darkness, light.

O Divine Master, grant that I may not so much seek to be consoled, as to console; not so much to be understood, as to understand; not so much to be loved, as to love. For it is in giving that we receive, it is in pardoning that we are pardoned, it is in dying that we are born again to eternal life.